TWELVE STEPS TO A NEW DAY

Ron Keller

A
JANET
THOMA
BOOK

THOMAS NELSON PUBLISHERS
Nashville

Published in Nashville, Tennessee, by Thomas Nelson, Inc., and distributed in Canada by Lawson Falle, Ltd., Cambridge, Ontario.

Scripture quotations are from the NEW KING JAMES VERSION of the Bible. Copyright © 1979, 1980, 1982, Thomas Nelson, Inc., Publishers.

Other references to the Scriptures are paraphrases of passages from J.B. Phillips; Today's English Version, Jerusalem Bible, and New International Bible Hyper-Bible.

To assure ultimate confidentiality none of the individuals referred to in this book are identified by their real names. Though the case studies are real, the situations are disguised and modified. These stories have been written and/or shared with the author orally so that they may be used to encourage others in their life journeys. The situations described have been gathered from small group gatherings all over the United States.

Library of Congress Cataloging-in-Publication Data

Keller, Ron.
     12 steps to a new day : an interactive recovery workbook for
spiritual growth / by Ron Keller.
          p.   cm.
    Includes bibliographical references.
    ISBN 0–8407–3460–3
     1. Twelve-step programs—Religious aspects—Christianity.
2. Spiritual life—Christianity. I. Title. II. Title: Twelve
Steps to a new day.
BV4596.T88A15 1993
248.8′6—dc20   92–28038
                                                CIP

Printed in the United States of America
1 2 3 4 5 6 7 - 99 98 97 96 95 94 93

To

_____

My mother, Vi,
in recognition of her life-long
love, prayer, support, and
continuous encouragement

Other Books by the Author

Twelve Steps to a New Day for Teens

CONTENTS

Acknowledgments

I am grateful for many people who have helped me
in the writing and editing of this book,
especially the following:

Nancy Keller, my wife, for her loving patience
and prayerful encouragement.

Janet Thoma for her consistent, positive, skillful,
and careful editing of this book.

Gail Steel, president of Prince of Peace Publishing, Inc.,
Burnsville, Minnesota, for her clear vision and
unwavering commitment to the success of this project.

DeWayne Herbrandson for enabling this project
to take place by serving as agent and consultant.

Sally Pearson for her timely visit from Cape Cod
to proofread and give evaluative feedback.

THE TWELVE STEPS FOR LIFE IN CHRIST

▼

Step 1: I admit that I am powerless over certain parts of my life and I need God's help.

> **Romans 5:6—We were powerless, when at just the right time, Christ died for us.**

Step 2: I am coming to believe that Jesus Christ came in a human body, that he is here with me now in Spirit, and that he has the power to change my weaknesses into strengths.

> **Colossians 1:15–17—Jesus Christ is the visible expression of the invisible God. All things were created by Him and for Him, and He holds all things in unity.**

Step 3: I turn my will and my life over to Jesus Christ, my Lord and Savior.

> **Galatians 2:20—I have been crucified with Christ. It is no longer I who live, but Christ who lives in me. And the life, which I now live in the flesh, I live by faith in the Son of God who loved me and gave Himself for me.**

Step 4: I begin honestly listing what I know and discover about myself: my strengths, weaknesses, and behavior.

> **Psalm 139:14, 23—I am wonderful and my soul knows this very well. Lord, examine me and know my heart. Probe me and know my thoughts. Make sure I do not follow harmful ways.**

Step 5: I am ready to honestly share with God and another person the exact nature of my strengths, weaknesses, and behavior.

> **James 5:16—Confess your sins to one another and pray for one another. In this way you will be healed.**

Step 6: I am entirely ready to have Jesus Christ heal all those areas of my life that need His touch.

> **Mark 6:56b—All those who touched Jesus were healed.**

THE TWELVE STEPS FOR LIFE IN CHRIST

▼

Step 7: I humbly ask Jesus Christ to change my weaknesses into strengths so that I will become more like Him.

> **1 John 1:9—If we acknowledge our sin, He is faithful and just. He will forgive us and purify us from everything that is wrong.**

Step 8: I make a list of the people I have hurt and become willing to go to them to mend the relationship.

> **John 13:34–35—By the love that you have for one another, the world will know that you are My disciples.**

Step 9: I make amends with the people I have hurt, except when to do so might bring harm to them or others.

> **Matthew 5:23–24—If you remember that your brother/sister has something against you, leave your offering there before the altar, go and be reconciled to your brother/ sister first and then come back and present your offering.**

Step 10: Each day I do a review of myself and my activities. When I am wrong, I quickly admit it. When I am right, I thank God for the guidance.

> **Galatians 6:4—Let each examine his own conduct.**

Step 11: To keep growing in my relationship with Jesus Christ, I spend time each day praying and reading the Bible. I will gather with others who do the same. I ask Jesus for guidance and the power to do what He wants me to do.

> **John 15:7—Remain in Me. If you remain in Me and My words abide in you, you may ask what you will and you will get it.**

Step 12: I am grateful that God is changing me through these Twelve Steps. In response, I will reach out to share Christ's love by practicing these principles in all that I do.

> **Matthew 25:40—Whatever you did to the least of My brothers/sisters, you did it to Me.**

THE TWELVE STEPS
FOR LIFE IN CHRIST

In October of 1987 I went to an unusually important Twelve-Step meeting. This one was a gathering of a variety of people who ranged in age from seventeen to seventy-four. None of them dressed alike. None of them looked alike. The younger folks were dressed in jeans and sweatshirts. Some of those a bit older came directly from work and wore suits.

It was not their church affiliation, beliefs, social class, age, hairstyle, or terminology that bound them together. These people were diverse in every way. On the surface, they seemed to have nothing in common.

Each participant had a personal issue to deal with. No one central problem or addiction brought the group together. In fact, no two people gathered there had the same concern. That in itself was unusual for a Twelve-Step gathering. Most groups focus on one issue. In the past, not many years ago, that issue was alcoholism.

What this group had in common was powerlessness. And that's what made the group work so well and so uniquely.

As soon as I met the first person in this room, I felt accepted. I could tell these people cared deeply about one another. And they were open to newcomers like me.

All Twelve-Step meetings are confidential. But with this group's permission, I share some of their first names and the issues that drew them to this gathering.

These ten people were gathered around three well-used, old, worn banquet tables. Several volunteers arrived half an hour early to push the tables together, make coffee, and set up a table for books. Clanging, cold, steel folding chairs were pulled around the tables as people straggled in. Coffee and tea and those now unpopular Styrofoam cups were available on an enamel catering cart.

It certainly wasn't the environment itself that drew these people here.

The meeting was held in the far side of a church library. Its familiar and comfortable surroundings made it ''home'' to many.

1

Participants in this meeting came from all over the metro area. Some had driven as far as twenty-five miles to be with each other. Most did this every week. They came here because this meeting gave them something no other meeting could.

The meeting began promptly at 7:30 P.M. Two leaders—one male, one female—led the group in some opening comments and prayer (see leader's guide, page 195 for a suggested format for support groups).

I was at this meeting on assignment: developing a training program for leaders. I was there to listen. I had been to more than forty other groups like this one in the past few months. I was in pursuit of answers to the question "What draws you here?" Shortly after the meeting began, I asked if some of them might be willing to share their answers with me.

Without hesitation they went around the table and openly shared their major struggles. There was no apparent embarrassment as they admitted to their issues.

"My name is Karen, I'm here because I abuse my children and I need help." After a moment of respectful hesitation, the next person stated his issue.

"My name is Ken. I have recently retired and I am depressed. I don't know what to do with my life. I need you all to help me. My wife is about ready to throw me out of the house."

"My name is Charles. I am an alcoholic."

"My name is Rita. I'm struggling with my marriage."

"My name is Tony. Two months ago, I was divorced from my wife of fifteen years. My whole life has fallen apart and I am trying to pull it back together."

"My name is Sally. I'm here because I want to grow in my relationship with God. I have been to many Bible studies, but I have never found anything like this group. This group helps me apply the Bible to real issues in my life."

"My name is Jo Ann. I came with Sally, but for different reasons. I don't know where I am with God. I had not found a good place to talk about this with anyone until I came here. Each time I come, I learn about how God is at work in people's lives. I am beginning to see Him at work in mine."

"My name is Tom. I pass."

It was my turn. They knew in advance that I was coming to the meeting, and I think they expected me to be a detached participant. "My name is Ron. I feel privileged to be here with you tonight. You seem to be such healthy and honest people. As you all went around the table and shared your struggles, I realized what a great thing you have going here.

"I am an ideal-a-holic. I think everything should work out right. I am sometimes blind and naive. I came from an alcoholic family. I am recovering from codependent behavior."

Now the room was quiet except for the occasional clearing of throats and the groaning of the dark ceiling beams, which extended across the width of the library.

It felt so good to be here. It was affirming to be with others who were willing to talk about what they were up against.

Is this what church *is? Is this the way it ought to be?* I wanted to ask out loud. *Is this the meaning of those passages that say we are to confess our sins to one another and carry one another's burdens? Is this what Jesus meant when He said, "Love one another as I have loved you,"* I thought as I leaned back in my chair and looked around the room.

Important things had just been shared, and everyone knew that. The silence demonstrated our respect for each other and the vulnerability that had been expressed.

I have learned that life is basically relationships. From my perspective the "good life" has little to do with material things. When my relationships are good, life is good. When my relationships are out of "synch," my whole life is out of synch. Only one unreconciled relationship can affect my attitude about everything and everyone else I am in touch with on any given day.

The Twelve-Step process is about relationships—with myself, with God, and with others. The Twelve Steps provide a step-by-step framework for gentle, continuous growth in each of these three relational areas. The Twelve Steps provide a measurable process for personal development. Quietly, deliberately, and gently the meeting moves along, touching each one who is ready to receive what is offered.

The Importance of the Twelve Steps and Twelve-Step Meetings

I have been participating in small-group meetings for more than thirty years. I cannot overstate the importance of those gatherings in my formation.

My first exposure to the Twelve Steps came when I was fifteen, through Al-Ateen, an organization for the children of alcoholic parents. I had heard about it long before I ever attended a meeting.

At that first meeting, I made a life-changing discovery. I discovered I was not weird or totally alone. Other kids were going through many of the same things in their families I was going through in mine. It was comforting to hear about the specific situations of other kids and how they handled each experience.

I'll never forget what Sarah said the first night I went to a meeting. "I never invite kids to come to my house anymore," she said, "because I don't know what will happen. I have been too embarrassed too many times. I can't take the chance of its ever happening again.''

That was my experience as well. Although I was not all that active in the group, I thought about it often and remembered that the group was there for me if I needed it.

What influenced me most about Al-Ateen was the adult sponsor, whose name was Jan. She had no children of her own. She was not married. She simply cared about kids enough to open her home to Al-Ateen on Sunday nights. She facilitated the meetings, but gave little advice or counseling. She was available to talk if we wanted to call her between meetings. She made a great impact on my life and became a model for my work with kids in Young Life.

Jan, the other kids in the group, and other adults that I met later helped me most. The principles of the Twelve Steps are simple. They are ''caught'' and not taught. I ''caught'' them at an early age without even knowing they had become a part of my life.

For thirty years, I have been involved in small groups. In college, I was part of several small groups and service organizations, including close friends in my Sigma Chi fraternity. The concept and importance of being in a small-group community are naturally part of who I am today. I have always longed to be close to a few people while still a part of a bigger body. I have always needed a core group to come back to.

After college, I was part of a small group through the Cursillo (a renewal movement in Catholic and Protestant churches). And then I participated in various groups for men, for Adult Children of Alcoholics (ACOA), and for those wishing to study the Bible.

In all these groups I have discovered several common reasons why people participate.

- ''I come here because I need support. I have so many struggles and issues to deal with, I need the support of others as I do my best to cope.''
- ''I need this group to encourage me. This is like a family for me. I leave my 'family' to go out to do my best as a father, husband, and manager. Right now, all of those areas are tough for me. This group encourages me to press on and do what is right.''
- ''This group is opening my eyes to areas of my life that I would not necessarily think about. They have helped me to see things that I need to change before I lose my family or job. I am thankful they have all quietly intervened in my life just by being who they are.''

The Twelve-Step Lifestyle Is for Everyone

Everyone has compulsions, addictions, or personal issues to be resolved. Alcoholics and drug addicts have an identifiable problem that has an identifiable "medication"—a chemical, liquor. In that sense, they are fortunate. Many of us, who are not alcoholics may not have behavior that merits traditional "treatment." However, our behavior may be so destructive that it surpasses the pain and damage caused by traditionally defined alcoholics.

We may go through our whole lives without ever knowing what feeds our discontent or gets in the way of genuine pleasure. We may frequently identify symptoms like loneliness, isolation, fear, lack of intimacy, rejection, or paranoia, but never get to the real problems. We may lick our wounds and bury battered emotions but never examine or treat the root of the trouble.

Paul tells us that we have all sinned and fallen short of the glory of God in Romans 3:23. John tells us that if we say we have no sin in us, we are deceiving ourselves and refusing to admit to the truth. He says in 1 John 1 that if we say that we have never sinned, we call God a liar (see vv. 8–10).

All of us sin. All of us need a Savior. All of us need help in living out this life.

Life can be difficult and challenging. For those trying to live a life following Christ, it can be even more trying. We need all the help we can get!

Through the years, I have made the following four observations:

1. Everyone lives with problems every day. These are often short-term problems: financial shortages, marital struggles, employment challenges, and family disruptions. We can cope with these problems because we know that we can solve them relatively soon. We live with these problems day by day and have grown accustomed to having them.

2. Everyone has problems that don't go away. These problems stay with us and can leave permanent scars. They can cause pain for years: death, divorce, fear, loneliness, and personality issues. They hang around and never seem to go away. Sometimes they don't seem serious enough to require "professional" attention, but the pain still prevents us from experiencing a full life. How can we handle these problems? The Twelve-Step framework gives us hope with these permanent struggles.

3. There is a way to live with these "permanent" problems. We can learn a way of life that makes life good even when it seems bad or falls short of our expectations.

4. No matter how hard life is, Jesus Christ has promised that He has come to be with us and to bring us a full life. We can have that life. The Twelve Steps can help us live a fuller, richer life in Christ.

The Twelve Steps for Life in Christ

Through Al-Ateen and other such organizations, I became friends with many people from the Alcoholics Anonymous and Al-Anon communities. I learned important life principles to supplement what I learned from my family at home. Some individuals in A.A. invested a great deal of themselves in me.

In college I was exposed to the idea of a personal relationship with Jesus Christ. Although I had grown up in a religious family and had been given great formational disciplines, I had not heard of this approach to life.

Shortly after college, through the Cursillo movement, the idea of knowing Jesus personally was confirmed. The Cursillo is the Spanish word for short course in Christianity. At a weekend retreat I totally surrendered my life to Jesus Christ. As a follow-up, in a small group with men I learned more about becoming one of Christ's disciples. In those early years of my Christian commitment, I saw many parallels between the Scriptures and the Twelve-Step process. I later learned that Alcoholics Anonymous' roots were in the Christian community. Bill Wilson, the cofounder of A.A., was a member of a support group that was part of the Oxford Movement, a renewal at Calvary Episcopal Church in New York City. At the twentieth anniversary of A.A. he introduced Sam Shoemaker, the rector of this church, as "the clergyman who in our pioneering time instructed certain of our older members in most of the spiritual principles which are today embodied in the Twelve Steps of Alcoholics Anonymous."[1] Early A.A. meetings were held in Shoemaker's church, and the meetings were structured like those of the Oxford groups.

As I participated in Al-Anon and other A.A. related groups and activities, I became more troubled about the use of the term *higher power*. This is the expression used in the Twelve Steps of A.A. to identify someone or something greater than ourselves. I felt it was inappropriate to use that term when as a Christian I knew Jesus Christ as the higher power. I told a good friend, who was a member of A.A., about my concern.

He expressed the same frustration. "I regret that I have not spoken more clearly about Jesus. I've had many opportunities all around the world in my work in A.A. to identify Jesus as my higher power. I am so sorry that I did not say His name more often," my good friend confessed.

---

[1]Alcoholics Anonymous Come of Age (New York: A.A. World Services, Inc., 1957), 253.

I had known him for years. He had shared a great deal of his life with me. He was suffering from cancer and feeling deep remorse about many aspects of his past.

"I urge you to speak straight and clearly about Jesus as your higher power. Until people meet Jesus, they will not find the peace and serenity they seek. Find ways to bring Him into this process," was his last challenge to me before he died.

I respect the need for the more generic term "higher power" in some groups. Many people in the first stages of recovery cannot comfortably refer to God or Jesus. But Sam Shoemaker meant to provide a recovery tool from sin for all people, especially those who wanted to live a life in Christ.

Many followers of Christ at that time apparently believed in what Paul said in 2 Corinthians 5:17: **"If anyone is in Christ, he is a new creation; old things have passed away; behold, all things have become new."** But they didn't know what it meant or how to apply it to their lives. Why were they having the same temptations as they had before they knew Christ? Why were they still behaving the same way? What did it mean to be a new creation but still have the same old bad behavior?

The Oxford Movement and its spinoffs were moving toward addressing these real, common human problems. But the church was not yet ready to embrace those who were suffering serious addiction—like alcoholics.

A few years after A.A. began, it partly separated itself from the Christian community, even though Sam Shoemaker remained active. A.A. almost had no choice, since the church did not yet understand what its good intentions were. A.A. took with it, in the separation, one major recovery tool Christians were about to discover: the Twelve Steps.

This, I think, was a tragic separation. It provided an easy way for Christians to label and dismiss alcoholics as the ones who had "that" problem, while they could conveniently live in denial about their own problems, which may, in fact, have been just as bad or worse.

"We all need two conversions," a good friend of mine once said. "The first is a total conversion to Jesus Christ and the spiritual life He provides. The second conversion is to becoming totally human, embracing and loving ourselves just as we are."

I am convinced that the Twelve-Step process provides the healthy platform to accommodate both conversions. I need both. The church needs both.

A direct confrontation finally motivated me to revise the Twelve Steps into the Twelve Steps for Life in Christ and to write books like the one you have in your hands.

In 1985 I was attending an Adult Children of Alcoholics meeting. We were discussing Step Three, and I mentioned that Jesus Christ is my Higher Power. One participant abruptly interrupted me. "We don't evangelize at these meetings. I feel very uncomfortable when you use that name here."

I respected this person's feelings, but I resented the fact that he could speak openly about his "higher power," the new-age god within him, but I could not make reference to Jesus.

In some cases, Twelve-Step groups have become platforms for evangelizing about "new" religions. Since no one is allowed to speak directly and clearly about Jesus Christ, some groups have become prey to weird theologies that make no direct reference to God. After that meeting I began to take seriously the assignment from my friend, to bring Jesus into this process. I have been working almost full time toward the use and development of these concepts and groups within the Christian community.

Followers of Christ who are in recovery are different. We know our Higher Power. We know there is power in His name. We know the need to articulate His name in prayer and publicly. I felt as if I were denying Jesus when I was in gatherings where I did not publicly state His name and instead used "higher power."

And members of Christian support groups (Bible study, parenting, Sunday school) can use the Twelve-Step process as a guide for their spiritual growth.

In the last several years, my associates and I have trained more than one thousand leaders to lead support groups throughout the country. Groups using these materials meet in more than thirty states. One church has twenty groups. We have begun several groups for pastors. Groups meet in prisons, in youth groups, and in public schools (after or before school begins).

"It's possible to be a healthy person and not have a relationship with Jesus Christ. In the long run that kind of health leads to nowhere" one pastor shared with me recently. "And it's possible to know Jesus Christ and not be healthy. I'm convinced that all people need a process like this to become healthy and whole emotionally, mentally, physiologically, and spiritually."

This process has become an important tool for many Christian churches. It offers "therapy" in the best sense of that word. It is a preventative program. It is the ultimate discipleship process. And it provides the genuine community that most Christians long for. This process brings healing, freedom, and fulfillment as nothing else can.

The Twelve Steps for Life in Christ on pages viii-ix represent this process.

Many of us live compartmentalized lives. We live one kind of life in one place and another kind of life in another. We keep secrets. We are forced to tell lies. "We are borderline schizophrenic," a workshop participant once said. "In some ways," she went on, "the church has taught us how to live this way. Because the church has not allowed us to be who we really are, we are forced to live two lives—our church life and our 'real' life. You are helping us find a way to connect these two lives.''

The Twelve-Step process helps us to be ''together'' people, the same on Monday night as we are on Sunday morning.

There is a need for the Christian community to provide platforms for people to be honest and bring their two lives together. The Christian community can provide safe places for people to talk about what life is really like for them. People must feel accepted for what they are, no matter what they do or have done.

Many Christians have run to the Alcoholics Anonymous community because it represents truth, honesty, openness, and acceptance. Christians who have not found that in the church have become sick of playing games and have given up hope.

No longer content to ''play church'' they have found their ''true fellowship'' in gatherings outside the church. The church has become a meaningless ritual for them, a self-serving, doctrinally preoccupied, sleeping giant that does not know how to care for and minister to the great needs of its people.

Through the years I have worked on ways to bring these two worlds together, the Christ-centered Christian world and the A.A. community. They both have much to give to each other.

This process provides the best of all worlds. It uses the proven, healthy Twelve-Step framework; it brings in the life-giving words of the Scriptures; and it provides a clear focus on the person of Jesus Christ, the Great Physician. This is what people are seeking; this is what the church can easily provide.

For many people, the church is really their last ray of hope. They cannot deal with their issues in the workplace. They come from families that are too dysfunctional to help them. The church is the one and only place that can provide a place and way for them to become congruent and whole.

It provides everything that people are looking for. One group participant stated, ''I was looking for a way to do self-improvement and improve my relationship with others. This process helped me with that and a whole lot more. I found a way to get rid of some of my past bad impressions about God. I now have a new and different relationship with Him because of this group.''

I have seen hundreds of lives quietly and gradually changed through this process. People become whole, healthy, confident, directed, and fulfilled by gently walking through these steps alone and/or with others.

How to use
This book

This is a workbook—your workbook. But it's not like any other you've ever used. You write your own story in this book. For many, this book has become their journal. As they write in this book from month to month and year to year, they see the progress they have made.

You don't need to rush through this book. This is a process to be involved in, not a program or curriculum to complete. Most people in A.A. work through the Twelve Steps many times.

This book has been designed for you to use it many times as well. On one step, you may only do one simple exercise and then move on to the next step. It's okay to leave some unfinished parts. Use the book long enough to get you into the flow of meditation. The goal is to use it as a tool to help you discover and experience a richer, fuller life.

When you go through the book the second, third, or fourth time, you will be surprised as you compare your new answers to those you had written earlier.

Each chapter deals with one of the Twelve Steps for Life in Christ and usually begins with a life story. At the end of this story you are sometimes asked to write some of your own responses to directed questions in a section entitled "How about You?" Such sections may be found in several places throughout the chapter.

This is usually followed by a section entitled "What the Bible Says" about this step. The book invites you to respond to several questions about the Bible texts in a section entitled "Doing This Step." Most passages are paraphrased to simplify them and make them easier to read. Rather than rush through all the passages, you might like to use one passage a day.

The last section of each chapter is entitled "Making This Step Your Own." This is an important section for application of the principles of each chapter into your own life situation.

I suggest you try to work on one step each week. After you've gone through

Step Twelve, return to Step One and renew the process at a deeper level. Each time you go through the Steps, focus on a word, phrase, or theme to help you through the day and week. It's not quantity or volume of content; it's quality and application that bring changes. Using this format, you would go through the steps about four times each year (forty-eight weeks).

The steps are not necessarily sequential. If possible, it is best to work one step after another but no one thoroughly completes one step before moving to another. You can jump in at any step and still benefit from the process. You do not have to begin with Step One. Even if you aren't familiar with Step One, you can benefit from the principles in Step Four. It is usually best to move through the Twelve Steps in twelve weeks and then return again to Step One.

Most people who leave one step to move on to the next leave it with an unfinished feeling. That's okay because this is a process, a life-long process. Growth in intimacy with yourself, with God, and with others is the ultimate goal of this book and process. Let the Holy Spirit lead and guide you through this challenge.

You will find that the first four steps have the most content and are likely to be the most challenging. Please do not be discouraged. If you do a little bit at a time, you will sense progress.

CHAPTER 1

I ADMIT THAT I AM POWERLESS

▼

Step 1:

I admit that I am powerless over certain parts of my life and I need God's help.

hen I was a teenager, the biggest problem I had to live with every day was my dad's drinking. He was an alcoholic. I never knew what to expect from him. Would he be drunk or sober? Did he mean what he was saying, or didn't he? Could I count on him or not? Would he embarrass me?

His alcoholism affected me in many ways. I was scared about him and his disease. I was afraid about what was happening to him, our family, and me. I felt I always had to be on guard. I missed having a father. When I was fifteen, my dad went into treatment. I remember how lonely I was. I was afraid he wouldn't come back home.

It took me a long time to figure out that I had no control over whether he'd come back or not. I realized there was nothing I could do about the situation. I couldn't change my dad. I could only change myself and the way I looked at things.

Step One helped me a great deal. It helped me to admit that I was powerless over these circumstances. I had no power to change my dad, myself, or my situation.

I thought about that feeling of powerlessness the night I visited that unique Twelve-Step group when the leader said, "Could we please look at Step One together, and could someone read Matthew 6:25–34?"

We read together, "I admit that I am powerless over my life and that I need God's help" and then proceeded to the reading in Matthew.

After the readings, the leaders divided us into small groups of four and then guided our discussion with questions. More and deeper sharing took place there as we all talked in depth about our issues and how we were dealing with them in light of Step One.

"This step helps me to admit my need for God's help. I am very powerless over my financial situation right now. I have not been irresponsible in spending, I simply don't have enough money to make ends meet. I have to let go of trying to make it all work. I have done my best, and now I need to trust God,'' one small-group participant shared.

After about forty-five minutes of small-group sharing, the leader invited us back to the larger group. "I would like to take a few minutes to reflect with you on Step One," she said. "This step asks me to honestly admit to who I am and the way I do things. It asks me to own my life, my lifestyle, and my problems. It asks me to face my life as it really is. This step urges me to surrender to God those things, circumstances, and people that I am powerless over."

Everyone listened intently as she went on. "This step invites me to slow down, gently shed my masks, and get into my heart. It invites me to come to God, who loves me and who longs to embrace me just as I am.

"This is not a self-help step or a self-help group. This group is for people who have had a taste of powerlessness and know that only God can help them.

"I have been working on this step almost every day this past week. Mostly, I have had to acknowledge my powerlessness over my health."

The leader was a thirty-five-year-old mother who had three children at home. She had cystic fibrosis.

"Sometimes I get bitter about my health. I think about how unfair it is that I have this disease. But one day at a time, I accept this problem and the impact it has on me and my family.

"Jesus loves to help. I know from my own experience. He asks, **'What do you want Me to do for you?'** in Luke 18:40. The first step in getting help is admitting that I am powerless and that I need God's help. This past week, I told Him I needed encouragement. He has given it to me.

"Tonight I need Jesus to come and be with me. I feel so weak and tired. Please pray with me that He will do it."

Several in the group spent a few minutes in brief, faith-filled prayers for this leader's expressed need. There was prayer for others in the room. The meeting was concluded. Most people hung around awhile longer. One woman suggested that she would be in touch with the leader. She was going to offer to baby-sit her children so that the mother could have a break.

As I walked to my car, I felt encouraged. I realized I had been in privileged company. People from a variety of backgrounds and educations came together on this night to share their lives with each other. What a great model it was. These people admitted that they were powerless over certain parts of their lives, which is a dilemma we all share.

Everyone Is Powerless over Something

At a recent dinner with friends, Jim asked, "What do any of you feel like you have power over?

"When I was younger," he went on, "I used to think I had power over everything. Now that I'm forty, I feel powerless over most things. I can ultimately do little about my health. I can't do anything to control my wife or kids. At work, I'm really at the mercy of the economy—I could lose my job any day. And I feel powerless about what is happening to our environment."

Ann, a participant in a Twelve-Step group, resented the word *powerless*.

"That word made me feel like I was supposed to give up, lie down like a rug and let everybody walk all over me. It made me feel like a loser. I have been abused and powerless many times in my life. I didn't want any more powerlessness. The word made me angry.

"And then I experienced its real meaning. I had reached the end of my rope with my son. He was eighteen and wanted to do life his way. I had been fighting to keep control of him. Gradually, I came to understand (as I still am) that I am powerless over him. He has his own life to live now. I have done my best for him. The powerlessness is not weakness but strength. I feel strong because I have chosen to surrender him to God."

Ann says she learned appropriate detachment. "Detachment is letting go, surrendering, and turning things over to God.

"Detachment is learning to take care of myself and being less concerned with the way my son is or what he does. Detachment, for me, is admitting powerlessness and accepting things as they are. Jesus Christ is the ultimate model of self-surrender and powerlessness for me."

We are all powerless over some thing, person, or situation that comes uninvited to our minds and seeks to dominate, control, or be in the center of our lives at the present moment. On the following pages you will be given a number of suggestions of people, situations, or things that might seek to "control" you. The key to overcoming these "addictions" is to identify the areas that you are powerless over (90 percent of the solution to any problem is proper diagnosis) and then admit them to yourself and someone else.

It's one thing to know our problems and addictions. It's quite another to admit that we have them and that we are powerless to change them.

Sometimes we blame others for the way we are. Our parents are common targets. But at some point in our lives, we need to take full responsibility for who we are. They did their part. We must now do ours.

When I was younger, I often used my father's alcoholism as an excuse. I had a reason to feel sorry for myself. I could blame him for some of the hard circumstances in my life. Fortunately, for the last five years of his life, my dad and I had a good relationship. I discovered many of his good qualities that I had not previously recognized. Our relationship had an unusually good ending, partly because I took responsibility for my own life and feelings. Eventually I came to realize that all of us face some hard circumstances. Until I went to Al-Ateen, I thought my situation was unusual. Now I know that all people have struggles.

I am still learning to live with the fact that I will always be powerless over certain parts of my life. Being powerless means I am without power, force, or energy. It means that I am weak, that I am not able to produce any effect or change. I am powerless over some of my own personality defects. I am judgmental. I'm a perfectionist. I'm an ideal-aholic (I think everything should be ideal). I am a workaholic.

I still admit, daily, my need for God's help. Life would be hopeless without God's intervention and ultimate control in my life. I need His help, today more than ever, in little and big things.

How about You?

To help you get started, please check which of the following areas seem to be problems, addictions, or challenges right now. You may check one or several—hopefully not all.

____ TV	____ Codependence (My needs are met by
✓ Feeling guilty	letting my life revolve around the wants
____ Work	and desires of others)
✓ Relationships	____ Taking care of myself
____ Sex	____ Being in a crisis
____ Chocolate	____ Being too spiritual
____ Food	____ Being preoccupied
____ Gambling	____ Fear
____ Smoking	____ Drugs
____ Sports	____ Videos/movies
____ Denial	____ Excitement
____ My dream	✓ Fantasies
____ Complacency	____ Caffeine: soda or coffee
____ Clothes	____ Myself
____ Being overwhelmed	____ My "helping" others
____ Lists like this	____ An affair (inappropriate emotional or
____ Being judgmental	physical bonding)
____ Shopping	____ Stability/security
____ Material things	____ Money
____ Upward mobility	____ Houses/property
____ Anxiety	____ Fatigue
✓ Fixing myself	____ Perfectionism

____ Controlling/manipulating   ____ Anger
_✓_ Stress   ____ Depression
____ A lifestyle
_✓_ FLESHFUL LUSTS   ___ _____

___ _____   ___ _____

Now do a quick overall assessment of where you are now. You need not show these written answers to anyone else unless you choose to do so.

Please answer quickly, with the first thing that comes to your mind.

1. My biggest problem right now is
     ____ My self confidence
     ____ My spouse
     ____ My child/children
     ____ My job
     ____ My salary
     ____ My peers
     ____ My relationship with God
     ____ Finances
     ____ My future
     _✓_ Secrets that I am carrying around
     ____ My past

     ___ _____
     ___ _____
     ___ _____

2. If I could change one thing in my life right now, it would be (For instance, I would change the way I look at things. I would stop trying to be in control.):

I WOULD CHANGE THE WAY I GIVE IN TO TEMPTATION I WOULD STOP TAKING THE SITUATION IN MY OWN HANDS AND LOOK TO GOD FOR HELP

3. The biggest mistake I've ever made is (I divorced my wife. I took the wrong job. I committed adultery.):

I GAVE IN TO LUSTFUL DIVERSE THAT LEAD TO SEXUAL SIN

4. When I think of my future I feel (Excited—I'm looking forward to our vacation. Scared—I'm worried about my job.)

SCARED — IM WORRIED ABOUT MY
RELATIONSHIP WITH OTHER, WITH A
FUTURE WIFE

Why?

BECAUSE I AM A SHAMED OF
WHAT I HAVE DONE AND I FEEL
LOWER THEN OTHER PEOPLE MY AGE

5. What gets me most excited right now is (a trip we'll be taking together, our retirement ideas, my weekly Bible study):

A TRIP.

Now think about your problems and your overall assessment as you read the following passage from the Bible. This reading is taken from the book of Matthew and is one of Jesus' most important teachings on how to live a healthy life. It is part of what is referred to as the Sermon on the Mount. It is also His classic address on "letting go," the dominant theme of the first step.

I, Jesus, am telling you not to worry about your life and what you are to eat, nor about your body and what kind of clothes you are to wear. Surely life means more than food, and the body more than clothing! Look at the birds in the sky. They don't sow or reap or gather into barns; yet the Lord feeds them. Are you not worth much more than they are?

Can any of you, for all your worrying, add one single minute to your life span? And why worry about clothing? Think of the flowers growing in the fields; they never have to work or spin, yet I assure you that not even Solomon in all his royal garb was robed like one of these. Now if that is how God clothes the grass that is there today and thrown into the furnace tomorrow, will the Lord not much more look after you, you of little faith?

So do not worry; do not say, "What are we to eat? What are we to drink? How are we to be clothed?" It is the pagans who set their hearts on all these things. Your heavenly Master knows you need them all. Set your hearts first on the Lord's kingdom and righteousness, and all these other things will be given you as well.

So, don't worry about tomorrow: tomorrow will take care of itself. Each day has enough trouble of its own (based on Matthew 6:25–34).

Now answer the following questions, which are based on this reading.

1. What is causing the most worry for you right now?

    ____ Relationships at home   ____ Friendships

    ____ Work   ✓ Temptations

    ____ Finances   ✓ Personal issues

    ____ Finishing this manuscript to meet the deadline

2. Describe a situation in your past in which you felt powerless (when I lost my job or when I went through a divorce):

    What did it feel like?

WHEN I LOST MY JOB, WHEN I COMMITTED A SIN

    What did you do about it?

I PRAYED FOR FORGIVNESS

3. In what area of your life do you feel powerless or out of control now? (I watch too much TV and I can't seem to stop. I am constantly preoccupied with thoughts about work.):

    How are you handling it?

I DON'T HANDLE IT, IT SEEMS TO OVER POWER ME

4. Have you asked for God's help? What's happened?

YES I HAVE BUT I GUESS I HAVE NOT FULLY SERENDERED IT TO GOD.

5. What is Jesus asking you to do in the reading on the previous page? (to seek His kingdom first and let everything be put in perspective):

DO NOT WORRY ABOUT TOMORROW

_____

_____

_____

6. In what specific areas of your life do you need God's help right now? (Today, I need help in my relationship with my wife—I need to be much more complimentary. Today, I need God's help to control my sexual desires and thoughts.):

Today's date _Dec 24/93_

1. _TODAY, I NEED GOD'S HELP TO CONTROL MY SEXUAL DESIRES AND THOUGHTS_

2. _TODAY I NEED GODS HELP IN MY RELATIONSHIP WITH LEANNE_

3. _TODAY I NEED GOD'S HELP IN MY DEVOTION WITH HIM_

4. _____

5. _____

What the Bible Says about Step One

   I admit that I am powerless over certain parts of my life and that I need God's help.

   Choose one passage from the selections given, and read it each day during the next week. Think about the passage by checking the statements below that reflect your feelings. Then write your own personal application of the passage as a final comment.

   1. Psalm 126:5–6: A verse taken from a song written by King David as his people were returning to Jerusalem. This is a promise for those who are presently feeling hopeless and weak. Joy will come, David says.

> **Those who sow in tears**
> **Shall reap in joy.**
> **He who continually goes forth weeping, . . .**
> **Shall doubtless come again with rejoicing,**
> **Bringing his sheaves with him.**

____ I don't sow tears.
____ I know this promise is true.

____ When I come to God with my powerlessness (and sometimes related sorrow), I come with the hope that He will someday replace my sorrow with joy.

____ _____

____ _____

____ _____

2. Psalm 23:1: In this well-known verse, David assures us that when the Lord is our Shepherd, we have all that we need. Step One urges us to admit our need for God.

> **The LORD is my shepherd;**
> **I shall not want.**

____ I can't say whether this is true for me or not
____ The Lord is my Shepherd. He has provided. He will provide. I trust Him.
____ It's really hard for me to trust anyone.

____ _____

____ _____

____ _____

3. Proverbs 3:5–7: Written by Solomon, a man thought to be the wisest king who ever lived, these verses instruct us to depend on God and not on our own abilities.

> **Trust in the LORD with all your heart,**
> **And lean not on your own understanding;**
> **In all your ways acknowledge Him,**
> **And He shall direct your paths.**
> **Do not be wise in your own eyes;**
> **Fear the LORD and depart from evil.**

_✓_ It is hard for me to give up control. I want to be in control.
____ Instead of trying to analyze situations or trying to make them go my way, I will trust the Lord with all my heart and let the outcome be in His hands.
____ It is hard for me to believe that I can't figure things out on my own and that I need to trust God for His judgment and intervention.
_✓_ It is hard for me to admit my powerlessness.

____ _____

____ _____

____ _____

4. Matthew 26:39: In one of Jesus' final hours on earth, he apparently was given a glimpse of the hell that he was about to go through. His agony drove him to pray the prayer below.

[Jesus] went a little farther and fell on His face, and prayed, saying "O My Father, if it is possible, let this cup pass from Me; nevertheless, not as I will, but as You will."

____ It was different for Jesus. He didn't really experience powerlessness.
____ I am thankful that I have a Savior who understands powerlessness.
____ I have been at this same point in my life. I know what this feels like.
____ Jesus encountered a trial that He chose to give over to His Father. In my powerlessness I, too, choose to give my life over to God.

____ _____

____ _____

____ _____

5. Romans 5:6, 8: Paul reminds his Roman friends that we are all powerless, sinners, and in need of rescue. Jesus came at just the right time, Paul says.

When we were still without strength, in due time Christ died for the ungodly. . . . But God demonstrates His own love toward us, in that while we were still sinners, Christ died for us.

____ Jesus came into the world at just the right time and for people who are powerless.
_✓_ I am a sinner. I need Jesus.
_✓_ Jesus Christ comes to help me in my powerlessness. He comes to me while I am in my human struggle to control my own life and future.

____ _____

____ _____

____ _____

6. Philippians 4:13: Paul is reminding the Christians in Philippi that they can

survive anything, including the lack of food and money. Step One lets us rest in truth that "we are weak, but He is strong."

I can do all things through Christ who strengthens me.

_____ I cannot rely on anyone else's strength.

_____ This passage has been true for me: I can do all things through Christ who strengthens me.

_____ When I try to deal with my kids on my own, I quickly get exhausted. When I ask for God's help, Christ strengthens me to endure all things.

_____ _____

_____ _____

_____ _____

Doing Step One

"The most difficult part of doing Step One for me is admitting to what leaves me powerless. I don't know why for sure, but it's real hard for me to admit to anything," one person in the group said.

"I was raised to solve my own problems. I was taught to depend on no one except myself. I am a self-reliant person. It's hard for me to trust God or anyone with my problems," another participant said.

"So what does all this admitting stuff mean to you?" a workshop participant asked me directly.

From my perspective, admitting to who we are and admitting to our need is essential to having a healthy life. Admitting, to me means several things:

1. It means I am willing to be who I am. I stop playing games. I get out of denial and stop pretending that I can do life on my own. I accept my humanness, my struggles and pain.

The first experience with admission that I can remember was when I accepted my powerlessness to change my dad or my circumstances. Up till that point, I thought I had the power to make a difference. I was living in denial.

2. Admitting means I can be where I am. I don't have to work so hard to be somewhere else. Most of my life has been spent in being where I thought I should be, rather than being where I am. This is a subtle form of denial.

3. Admitting is surrendering. I can let go, turning the struggle over to God and letting the outcome be His.

It can be reflected in a prayer like this: *God, this is what life is like for me right now. Here is what I am feeling. This is who I really am. I am coming in for a landing here. Thank you for giving me the courage to be who I am.*

4. Admitting is a form of trusting. The only way I can really make progress in life is to learn to trust myself, others, God, and my circumstances. That means saying to myself, *The way life is for me now, is the way life is supposed to be for me now.*

5. Admitting is accepting things as they are, not as I would like them to be. Before I can do anything to change things, I need to accept them as they are.

When I do not accept reality, I am living in denial. I am looking for a fix before I have dealt with why the problems are there in the first place. This step allows me to relax and let God do what needs to be done without me and my intervention.

6. Admitting means I confess my sins, failure, and need. I sometimes resent my powerlessness. I would like to be in better control of some of the events in my life. This is sin. It is competing with God. Only God can be God. He is ultimately in control.

7. Admitting is rediscovering that Jesus Christ is with me and that He will never leave me, as He has promised. He is present, whether I like it or not. The sooner I admit to His presence and acknowledge it, the healthier I become.

As I made each of these seven points in the group, the participants shared their own experiences and feelings. Many of them had experienced this admission and shared the benefits they enjoyed from living this way.

"I find relief, peace, and serenity when I admit to who I am and to what is happening in my life. I get really stressed out when I try to deny things," one young woman said.

"I feel pressure build up inside me when I try to exercise my own power and fix things. When I admit to my powerlessness, I feel relief," said another.

Making Step One My Own

This section provides you with a format for integrating your feelings, responses to questions, and what you learned from this step, the Scriptures, and in your group meetings.

Date, day, and time of your writings:_____

1. At this point in my life, the major area that I am working on (For instance, I have discovered that I want to be in control of my life. It is hard for me to admit powerlessness or weakness. I have become aware of how much influence my father's workaholism has had on me.):

_____

_____

2. Major insights I was given into my life through this step (By listening to others, I learned that it is okay to be who I am; I don't need to play games or pretend.):

_____

_____

_____

_____

3. The scriptural passage that spoke to me most clearly in this step (Matthew 6 tells me not to worry about tomorrow because today has enough trouble of its own.):

_____

The one word that has been most important to me in this chapter (the word *surrender,* to let go):

_____

_____

4. The major discovery about Jesus Christ that I was given in this step (I had forgotten that Jesus was human like us. He, too, had to surrender His life and do what His Father wanted.):

_____

_____

5. The strongest feeling I have as I have worked this step (Relief—it's okay for me to be human.):

_____

6. The action I feel called to take as a result of working this step (I am now going to work at being more relaxed and less in control.):

_____

7. The good news for me in this step and these passages (I am acceptable as I am even when I am weak.):

_____

CHAPTER 2

I CAN'T CHANGE MYSELF— BUT GOD CAN

▼

Step 2:

I am coming to believe that Jesus Christ came in a human body, that He is here with me now in Spirit, and that He has the power to change my weaknesses into strengths.

hen Ken lost his job, he felt hopeless about his future. He was worried about how his family would survive without his income.

Ken had grown up in a family with a very strong work ethic. In his relations, the important people were the ones who had accumulated wealth. "They were the ones," he said, "who had power and influence."

"What I am learning is that my value comes from what I do. In my family no one ever asks or thinks about who you are; they want to know what you do, and then they make up their minds about whether you're an important person or not," Ken went on.

"They think I am valuable when I have power over others. If you don't have money or power, you aren't a very important person in our family."

Many in Ken's group were nodding their heads. They knew what he was talking about.

This was a new discovery for Ken. He had felt this stuff but had never before said it out loud. In the last four months he was learning how to say these things in this group. As he said them, he felt better about himself.

"So here I am without a job. I feel worthless. I'm embarrassed to let my parents know that I've lost my job. I'm discovering that what I think of myself is based on my family's material standards. I don't like that. I want to change it. I know I need to change it."

Over a period of weeks, Ken unwrapped parts of his life and got to the heart of some of his repressed feelings. It became clear that his self-image was based on performance. If he could do things well and accomplish many things, he felt acceptable to himself and others.

Ken, like many adults, has been convinced by the cultural standards of our time that we are lovable when we wear a certain type of clothing, have a specific type of education, know certain people, own specific things, live in a specific neighborhood, and have a high income.

These cultural standards have been handed down from one generation to the next. For healthy relationships to take place in the family, someone will need to break and then change this pattern. The Scriptures teach us that **"For by grace you have been saved through faith, and that not of yourselves; it is the gift of God, not of works, lest anyone should boast"** (Eph. 2:8–9). The world teaches us to earn our salvation (and everything else). The Scriptures teach us that all of these are gifts.

Changes do not come easily. When we've been "programmed" in a specific way from early childhood on, it will not be easy to "deprogram."

The easy "fix" for Ken would have been to rush out and keep trying to get another job. To get healthy, Ken needed more than that. Ken needed to deal with the hard issues in his life, which prevented him from having a healthy self-image whether he had a good job or not.

Others in Ken's group shared what God was doing in their lives to transform their weaknesses.

"I used to feel lonely all the time. I hate being lonely. But God has come to me, and He is changing my loneliness," Tom said.

"I've had major health problems," Joan said. " I've taken each physical weakness to the Lord and He has healed or He is healing me.

"For months I had been exhausted. I know part of that came from my busy schedule, but a part of it was unexplainable. I needed energy and vitality. I asked God for His help, and He gave it to me," Alice said.

In each of these people's lives, Jesus Christ is doing miracles. They give the credit to Him because they have tried to change themselves and they have failed time and time again. Then He has come to help. He has the power to change them.

What about You?

Step Two—I am coming to believe that Jesus Christ came in a human body, that He is here with me now in Spirit and that He has the power to change my weaknesses into strengths—is an important step for those who have doubts about where God is in their lives. Sometimes problems are so great that it hardly seems possible that God cares. Step Two lets us say with integrity, "Where is God in all this?"

Step Two affirms three simple truths:

1. Jesus Christ did miracles when He was here in human form.
2. Jesus Christ is the same yesterday, today, and forever.
3. Jesus will do miracles in our time.

1. Jesus Christ Did Miracles When He Was Here in Human Form

If you need healing, there's no better place to look than in the first four books of the New Testament—Matthew, Mark, Luke, and John. It's often said that these books tell the story of the Great Healer. And that Great Healer is Jesus Christ.

Consider this story, which is just one of many.

There was a wedding at Cana in Galilee. Mary, the mother of Jesus, was there, and Jesus and His disciples had also been invited. When the hosts ran out of wine at the wedding, Jesus' mother said to the servants, "Do whatever he tells you."

There were six stone water jars standing there. Each could hold twenty or thirty gallons. Jesus said to the servants, "Fill the jars with water," and they filled them to the brim. "Draw some out now," He told them, "and take it to the steward."

They did this. The steward, who knew nothing about what had happened, tasted the water, and it had turned into wine. He called the bridegroom and said, "People generally serve the best wine first and keep the cheaper sort till the guests have had plenty to drink; but you have kept the best wine till now."

This was the first of the signs given by Jesus. He let His glory be seen, and His disciples believed in Him (based on John 2:1–11).

After reading about Jesus Christ changing the water into wine I

____ feel discouraged. This incident was for His lifetime only.

____ am hopeful. If He can change water into wine, He can change my weaknesses into strengths.

____ wish He would do a major miracle in my life.

____ wish I could have been at the wedding party.

2. Jesus Christ Is the Same Yesterday, Today, and Forever

This is the promise that Jesus gave to all of His followers in Hebrews 13:8. He will never change. He has the same ability and power today as He did when He expressed Himself in human form.

He created the universe. All that has been created was created by, for, and through Him. He expressed Himself by taking on human form. He came for sinners and the lost and those who are sick.

He does the same today. He comes for the needy. He forgives sin. He finds the lost, and He heals those who are sick.

And He promised that He will be this way forever. He will never change. Everything else around us may change. Jesus Christ will never change.

He said He is the Alpha and the Omega, the beginning and the end, in Revelation 22:13.

Before any of us can take Step Two, we must know who Jesus is. He told us Himself in the Bible. After reading each statement below, write a brief comment about how it might apply to your life right now.

1. Jesus said, **"I am the bread of life"** (John 6:35).
(For instance, I trust that Jesus will feed me physically and spiritually.)

_____

_____

2. Jesus said, **"I am the light of the world"** (John 9:5).
(For instance, Jesus shines into the darkness of my life and brings light so that I can see more clearly who I am and what my circumstances are.)

_____

_____

3. Jesus said, **"I am the resurrection and the life. He who believes in Me, though he may die, he shall live"** (John 11:25).
(For instance, because Jesus was resurrected from death, I, too, will be resurrected someday and live with Him in heaven forever.)

_____

_____

4. Jesus said, **"I am the way, the truth, and the life. No one comes to the Father except through Me"** (John 14:6).
(For instance, Jesus is the way in life; He is the truth and He gives me life. I come to God the Father through Him.)

_____

_____

5. Jesus said, **"I am the true vine"** (John 15:1).
(For instance, I am a branch. Jesus is the vine. He supports me.)

_____

_____

3. Jesus Will Do Miracles in Our Time

After His life on earth Jesus continued to do miracles through His followers in the early church as recorded in various passages in the book of Acts. All through history, believers have affirmed His miraculous intervention in their lives.

Today many people speak convincingly of miracles they have experienced. Those three people in Ken's group were just a few of the thousands of people in groups throughout the country who tell the same story: "I asked God for His help, and He gave it to me."

We can't do anything about certain parts of our lives, but Jesus Christ can. If He can change water into wine, He can change the minor difficulties we have.

Jesus Christ has the power to change our weaknesses into strengths.

____ That's the best news I've heard in years; I know I can't do it by myself.

____ I need His help and all the help I can get.

____ I don't believe this. I feel like a hopeless case. I know in my head that Jesus majors in hopeless cases, but I don't believe it in my heart.

____ I want to believe this, but I have no evidence up to this point in my life.

What the Bible Says about Step Two

I am coming to believe that Jesus Christ came in a human body, that He is here with me now in Spirit, and that He has the power to change my weaknesses into strengths.

Choose one passage from the selections given and read it each day during the next week. Think about the passage by checking the statements below that reflect how you feel. Then write your own personal application of the passage as a final comment.

1. John 6:28–29: The crowds had jumped into several boats and followed Jesus after he had multiplied the fishes and loaves. He told them not to work for food that cannot last. **"They said to Him, 'What shall we do, that we may work the works of God?' Jesus answered . . . , 'This is the work of God, that you believe in Him whom He sent.'"**

____ For me, believing in Jesus comes easy.

____ Believing in Jesus is a real struggle for me.

____ I believe with my mind, but I do not trust Jesus with my heart and daily life.

____ I want to trust in Jesus Christ with all my heart.

____ Trusting that His will is being done is very difficult for me when I cannot make ends meet each month.

____ _____

____ _____

____ _____

2. Luke 10:23, 24: Jesus tells His disciples that the good news, His presence as Savior of the world, is revealed to the simple. **"And He turned to His disciples and said privately, 'Blessed are the eyes which see the things you see; for I tell you that many prophets and kings have desired to see what you see, and have not seen it, and to hear what you hear, and have not heard it.'"**
____ I can see Jesus clearly. I know who He is and I see Him at work in my life.
____ I want to see Jesus more clearly. I am open to hearing His voice.
____ I am afraid to open my eyes to Jesus.
____ I am so grateful that God has given me the eyes to see who Jesus is.
____ Even though I do not see Him clearly, I do have faith in His presence and His ability to help me today.

3. 1 John 5:11–13: In his first letter, John reminds his readers that Jesus Christ came to deliver us from sin, self-destruction, and death. He not only has the power to change my weaknesses into strengths, He has the power to give me eternal life. **"And this is the testimony: that God has given us eternal life, and this life is in His Son. He who has the Son has life; he who does not have the Son of God does not have life. These things I have written to you who believe in the name of the Son of God, that you may know that you have eternal life."**
____ I still believe eternal life is something that I earn.
____ I still believe eternal life is a reward I get for avoiding certain things.
____ I believe I have been given eternal life in Jesus Christ.
____ I am afraid of this whole idea.
____ I know that I have eternal life because of what Jesus has done for me. This gift He has given me regardless of my weaknesses.
____ _____
____ _____
____ _____

Doing Step Two

Step Two lets us be where we are. It does not push us to say something that isn't true for us. It lets us slow down, evaluate where we are, and be honest with ourselves and in a group. It is a reminder that this is a process, not an overnight fix. We are gradually coming into a deeper faith in Jesus Christ. We are gradually getting a better understanding of what His coming and presence can mean to us.

Where are you in this process? Check the statements below that reflect your feelings:

1. The beginning of Step Two says, "I am coming to believe."
_____ I fight this. I do not want to believe. I want to see; I am a doubter.
_____ I am a doubter, but I want this part of my life to change.
_____ This is true for me. I recognize that I am in the process of becoming a stronger believer.
_____ I feel secure in my faith. My life experience has taught me that I can believe.

2. That God, Creator of the universe, came to His own creation as a human person is:
_____ Beyond my comprehension
_____ I've never really thought about this much.
_____ What difference does it make that God came as a human person?
_____ This is the truth and I want to learn how to respond in worship and gratitude.

3. Jesus Christ is with me now in Spirit.
_____ This makes no difference in the way I live my life, really.
_____ I've never really thought about it.
_____ I've always believed this.
_____ I believe this, but this truth doesn't make much difference in the way I live my life.
_____ I want to learn and do more about this.

4. To me, the Holy Spirit is:
_____ A doctrine.
_____ A spirit, unidentifiable and unknowable.
_____ A "thing."
_____ A universal "idea."
_____ The Holy Spirit is a Person who comes to reside within those believers who call on Him: **"Your heavenly Father [will] give the Holy Spirit to those who ask Him"** (Luke 11:13).

Step Two assures us that it is okay to be moving toward belief, moving forward, knowing that we will never completely arrive. We are "coming to believe." This means we are on the way. No one expects us to have perfect faith or be perfect persons. Our faith is perfected as our relationship with God grows and our ability to trust the Lord is strengthened through experience.

In the spaces below, write about an experience. Share it with your group if you are part of a group and are comfortable doing so.

1. Describe a situation or time in your life when you became confident that Jesus Christ is with you in spirit.

_____

_____

_____

2. In what areas has Jesus Christ changed your weaknesses into strengths?

_____

_____

_____

The following article affirms the power and impact that Jesus' life has on people in all of history.

One Solitary Life

Here is a man who was born in an obscure village . . . the child of a peasant woman. He grew up in another obscure village . . . He worked in a carpenter shop until He was thirty . . . and then for three years He was an itinerant preacher.

He never wrote a book . . . He never held an office . . . He never owned a home . . . He never had a family . . . He never went to college . . . He never put his foot inside a big city . . . He never traveled more than two hundred miles from the place where He was born . . . He never did one of the things that usually accompany greatness . . . He had no credentials but Himself . . . He had nothing to do with this world except the naked power of His divine manhood.

While He was still a young man, the tide of popular opinion turned against Him . . . His friends ran away. One of them denied Him . . . He was turned over to His enemies . . . He went through the mockery of a trial . . . He was nailed to a cross between two thieves . . . His executioners gambled for the only piece of property He had on earth while He was dying . . . and that was His coat.

When He was dead, He was taken down and laid in a borrowed grave through the pity of a friend.

Nineteen centuries have come and gone, and today He is the centerpiece of the human race and the leader of the column of progress.

I am far within the mark when I say that all the armies that ever marched . . . and all the navies that were built . . . and all the parliaments that ever sat, and all the kings that ever reigned put together have not affected the life of people upon this earth as powerfully as has that One Solitary Life.

(Author unknown)

This second step, as described in "One Solitary Life," is the core of the Christian faith. God came to human beings as a human being. This is a crucial, pivotal, radical expression of love. This is grace, pure and rich. This is the greatest event in history.

Making Step Two My Own

This section provides you with a format for integrating your feelings, your responses to questions, and what you learned from this step, the Scriptures, and your group meetings.
Date, day, and time of your writings:_____

1. At this point in my life, the major area that I am working on (For instance, I know I need help in accepting the fact that God is present and involved in my painful issues.):

_____

_____

2. Major insights I was given into my life through this step (I forget that God is present with me in this life. I don't even think about this.):

_____

_____

_____

_____

3. The scriptural passage that spoke to me most clearly in this step (As we read the story of changing water into wine, I realized that could be me. I could be changed too. Jesus could make something more of my life.):

_____

The one word that has been most important to me in this chapter (the word weakness—He will turn my weaknesses into strengths):

_____

_____

4. The major discovery about Jesus Christ that I was given in this step (He is not only my Savior for eternal life; He is with me now and cares deeply about all of the concerns of my life.):

_____

_____

5. The strongest feeling I have as I have worked this step (excitement about having some things in my life finally get changed):

_____

6. The action I feel called to take as a result of working this step (Let God do the changing in me—stop trying to do it on my own; it doesn't work anyway.):

_____

7. The good news for me in this step and these passages (God has the power to change me.):

_____

CHAPTER 3

SURRENDER
LEADS TO
SERENITY

Step Three:

**I turn my will and my
life over to Jesus Christ,
my Savior and Lord.**

or several weeks I had been experiencing numbness and tingling on the left side of my body. I have generally been in good health. I am able to run three miles three times each week.

Suddenly, these pains and sensations came out of nowhere, and my doctor, after doing all the tests he could, sent me to a neurologist. The neurologist ordered an overwhelming series of tests. I didn't know the body could be checked in so many ways.

First in the series were numerous blood tests, all of which turned out to be negative. These were followed by an EMG (shock and needles); a brain wave test; and two MRIs—a brain scan and a neck scan.

Hard as the test was, I had a great experience with the EMG. The attending technician was one of the friendliest young women I had ever met. After a brief explanation of the process that she was about to put me through, she said, "You can do this test. The Lord will be with you." Her encouragement prompted me to ask if she was a Christian. "I've been a believer since 1980," she said, "but I've *really* been a believer since 1988."

"What happened then?" I asked.

"I was doing a test like the one I'm doing on you," she said as she stuck another needle in my thigh.

"The guy lying on this table had AIDS. He told us. Our whole office knew it. I was praying for him the whole time I was administering this test. And then I did a crazy thing. I poked myself with a needle that I had just taken out of his arm. I have never done anything like this before in my whole career."

She hesitated for a few moments as tears rolled down her face. "For six months, my life was hanging in the balance. I was immediately put on a medication to counteract the HIV virus, a medication that really messed up my body. And for that six months we had to wait to know for sure whether I had been infected with AIDS. My husband and I spent many nights on our knees. I totally surrendered my life to Jesus Christ. I gave Him everything I had. I learned to live life one day at a time and I'm still doing it.''

As she finished the tests on me, she told me the good news that up to this point she is still negative.

For several days before the MRI tests, my wife, Nancy, and I had been told about the two worst possibilities: (1) a malignant brain tumor (assuming they could in fact find a brain!) or (2) multiple sclerosis. ''Anything other than these two would be good news,'' Nancy said.

We both spent three nights ''dreaming'' about what might happen should either of these be the diagnosis. All we could do, with each thought, was surrender, turn my body over to Jesus Christ, and ask Him to do what must be done. I felt much liberation as I was able to let go of the outcome of the tests and my future—even if that future meant major surgery or confinement to a wheel chair.

I had heard about the infamous MRI ''tunnel'' and how difficult it is for claustrophobic people. Fortunately, I was not one of those people. My body was small enough to fit comfortably into the tight space.

When I lay helpless inside the ''tunnel'' for the MRI brain scan, I realized how helpless I was. I could do nothing but lie there and ''let go''—let the technicians do what they needed to do; let the doctor do what he needed to do. All I could do was surrender and lie still. I survived the experience by imagining I was in the sleeping quarters of a great sailboat. I can tolerate anything related to sailing.

''The good news is you have a brain and it's fine,'' the neurologist reported three days after the test. ''You have no tumor and no multiple sclerosis. The bad news is we still don't know what is causing these problems in your body, and so the testing will continue'' (translated, the torture will continue).

The doctor has since discovered that I have three degenerating disks in my neck, and these have caused the pain, the numbness, and the tingling. I have had to stop running and learn ways to live with this until or when I will need surgery, which will be never if I can do anything to avoid it.

I have realized how terribly vulnerable and fragile I am. At any moment I could need surgery, be in a wheel chair, or face death. All of these are simple reminders that my life has lasting value only when it is committed to Jesus Christ and lived moment by moment for Him. He is using all of these daily experiences to draw me closer to Himself.

Many other challenging trials have taken me back to the same place: if I am to enjoy my life, I must give it to Jesus Christ.

One of the groups gathered in our small living room on Monday nights.

Having met weekly for several years, we graduated to a monthly meeting and really looked forward to being together.

As we looked at Step Three, several people described why they were afraid of taking this step.

"I am afraid," Sonya said, "that nothing will happen if I give my life to Jesus Christ. I would be devastated if God doesn't do something to respond to me when I give Him my life."

"I don't want to get religious," Fred said. "I've been around too many Jesus freaks, and they turn me off. I don't want to become like that, so that's why I hold back."

"Same with me," Johanna said. "I don't want to be a zealous missionary in Africa, and I have this feeling that if I give my life to God, He'll send me there. I don't want to go, so I hold back."

"God may or may not make great demands on our lives. It is His right to do so. We are His possession," one of the group leaders said.

"The core problem in life for all of us," she went on, "is that we ultimately want to be our own gods. We play god. We want to run our own lives. Even if we do it poorly—running our lives right into the ground—we still prefer to be in control."

The message from our culture is simple and consistent: Be in control. "If you stay in control," our culture says, "you will have happiness, success, and prosperity."

"There are two fundamental realities in life," my friend's poster says. "Number one—there is a God. Number two—you are not Him." Step Three is a simple reminder of those fundamental realities.

You probably identified some of the items on the list of addictions when you made Step One. Addictions are often our gods. We use them to fill the natural void inside us, which should be filled by God.

How can we displace these gods?

I think Jesus gave us two very clear answers:

1. You must become like little children. The kingdom of heaven is for those who become children.

My son, Jonathan, is one of my main mentors. I used to think I would learn most from older people. That was at one time true. Now, I need to let younger people like Jonathan help me rediscover what life is really all about.

Jonathan has a healthy trust in his parents and adults. He assumes that they will do what they say. He looks forward to their following through on their words.

Jonathan also has plenty of fun. He doesn't work at it—having fun comes easily for him. He is carefree and can enjoy life because he doesn't let the cares of this world affect him too much. He knows how to keep life's cares in perspective.

Jonathan likes adventure and surprises. He likes to play games and ask questions about what we'll do next.

He lives for the moment. Except for an occasional spurt of concern for tomorrow, Jonathan's life is focused on totally enjoying this moment of life.

Jonathan is dependent upon his parents, family, and God. He knows that intuitively. He knows that he needs to rely on us for the basic things in life, and in his own way, he accepts this dependence as reality.

By simple trust and healthy dependence on God like Jonathan's, we displace those other "gods" who seek to hold us captive.

2. Jesus said, "You must be born again" (be born from above). This is the second way to displace foreign gods. There's a story in the gospel of John that describes this more thoroughly.

A wealthy Pharisee named Nicodemus was one of the first people to be born again. He was a Pharisee, a leader in the Jewish religion. He came to talk with Jesus one night and said, "Rabbi, we know that You are a teacher who comes from God. No one could perform the signs that You do unless God was with Him."

Jesus answered, "I tell you the truth, unless a man is born from above, he cannot see the kingdom of God."

Nicodemus said, "How can a grown man be born? Can he go back into his mother's womb and be born a second time?"

Jesus replied, "Unless a man is born through water and the Spirit, he cannot enter the kingdom of God" (based on John 3:1-5).

How about You?

Check the statements that indicate your response to this story.

1. I think Nicodemus was
____ a used chariot salesman who was fed up with his lifestyle and sought Jesus for a better way of life.
____ a leading Jew who came to Jesus by night because he was a spy for the Pharisees.
____ a man who had heard just enough about Jesus that he wanted to meet Him face to face to check out whether Jesus might be the one he should give his life to.
____ a person who was drawn by the Holy Spirit to enter into a relationship with Jesus Christ.

_____ I can identify with Nicodemus. He was a man a lot like me in the following ways (For instance, He was curious about Jesus; He was afraid his friends might know about his curiosity so he went to see Jesus at night):

_____

_____

2. When I read "turn your will over to Jesus Christ," I am reminded of experiences in my own life when I
_____ have fought this idea.
_____ resented this notion that God wants my will and life.
_____ have resisted the idea of turning my will over to Jesus Christ.
_____ knew exactly what it meant to turn my will over to Jesus Christ but still did not do it.
_____ did this and continue to do it.

_____

3. Different denominations and schools of theology have their own expressions and cultural terms that try to grasp the meaning of Jesus' expression "unless a person is born from above, he cannot see the kingdom of God." My experience with this expression has been that
_____ I have been born from above (born again).
_____ I want to be born from above (born again) but don't know what it's all about.
_____ I guess this rebirth happened for me somewhere along the line.
_____ I think this rebirth happened for me in my confirmation experience.
_____ I feel like I am on the verge of some kind of spiritual rebirth right now.
_____ I am open to rebirth but afraid.

_____

4. Check the expressions below that best describe your understanding of being "born again."
_____ This is a process. It is something that is still happening to me now.
_____ Being born again marks the beginning of a new life, a fresh start, a turning point when I receive God's love.
_____ This is the beginning of a new relationship with God. I see what God has done and is doing in my life.
_____ This is the key to understanding the Scriptures.
_____ This experience happens to each person in a different way.

_____ This is something that all adults must decide about and experience on their own.

---

5. From my experience, rebirth is most like
_____ conversion (being changed, transformed, returning to God).
_____ repenting (a change of my mind and heart toward God; a change of my direction; a transformation of my thoughts, attitudes, and outlooks).
_____ renewal (regeneration, restoration, re-creation, rejuvenation, being revived).
_____ reconciliation (being reunited with God at His initiative and invitation).

According to this passage, rebirth is not an option. Jesus says "unless a person is born from above, he cannot see the kingdom of God." This rebirth happens at God's initiative. God begins this process and accomplishes it by grace. We are the recipients of His acts of grace and kindness. The process begins and ends with God. It's part of what I have defined as the surrender cycle.

The Surrender Cycle

The surrender cycle is a process of becoming a whole person. This cycle has five phases: awareness, admission, struggle, surrender, and serenity (see diagram, page 51).

In all of these phases, our choices are responses to Jesus' question addressed to the paralyzed man at the pool of Bethsaida: "Do you want to be whole?"

To become whole, we need to be aware of our condition. We need to become more aware of our "addictions," compulsions, and personality traits. Because many people live in denial, they are not totally aware of their true condition. They avoid reality and stay in denial by watching TV or medicating their pain with chemicals, sex, or hyperactivity.

"For twenty-five years I was a driven man," Joe said. "At the expense of my relationship with my wife and children, I was determined to be successful in my work. Until I became aware that I am a bona fide perfectionist, nothing in my life could change."

His awareness came through pain. The older he got, the more anxious he felt about his life and career. He got physically sick from his psychological problems. He was headed for a breakdown until his wife finally intervened. She gave him an ultimatum: Change your lifestyle or you'll lose your family. At this point he took the necessary steps to change his life pattern.

Awareness comes in a variety of ways. Some become aware through prayer, loving companions who speak the truth to them, circumstances, and the Scriptures. In one of his letters, John wrote: **"If we say we have no sin in us, we are deceiving ourselves and refusing to admit the truth . . . to say that we do not sin is to call God a liar. But if we acknowledge our sins, God, who is faithful and just, will forgive us our sins and cleanse us from all wrong"** (based on 1 John 1:8–10).

"All have sinned and fall short of the glory of God," Paul tells us in Romans 3:23.

All of us have a need to become more aware of who we are and how our behavior affects us and our relationships with God and others. This is difficult for most of us because we are creatures of habit. We are so well established in our patterns and lifestyles that we assume they are all okay—until something major happens to wake us up.

If we want to become whole, we must be alert to ourselves, others, and the circumstances in our lives.

Awareness is the first phase of becoming whole. Admission to ourselves, God and another person is the second.

As Joe began to work on his perfectionism with a professional counselor and in a group using this book, he discovered a long line of perfectionists in his family. He had always thought his family was ideal, but he was now discovering that many unspoken and unhealthy rules had been imposed on him.

He began to admit to himself and others the facts about his life. His family was not as ideal as he thought. It was not a bad family on the surface. But beneath the socially acceptable signals, there was much unaddressed turmoil and frustration.

For years, he had pretended that his father and grandfather had no flaws, foibles, or problems, that they were "perfect." They were his heroes and models. Now Joe was moving out of denial and admitting that they were human and had problems just like everyone else. This admission gave him the freedom and permission he needed to explore how their issues, subdued as they might have been, had affected him, especially in his perfectionism.

It was his verbal admission of this compulsion that helped him assess his life realistically. He then let go and let God go to work on changing this deficiency in his life.

"My whole identity is based on how well I can perform. I feel good about myself only when I am doing something really good—and better than others can do it," Joe said. As Joe talked openly, the perfectionism lost its intense power over him. He realized he was not alone as others shared about performance-based identity. He felt hopeful about the changes that could take place in his life. Others in his group had walked the path before him and represented hopeful light at the end of the tunnel.

The psalmist apparently had a similar experience with denial and then admission. Perhaps many of the great saints and biblical heroes were more human than we recognize. As I have examined their lives more closely through the years, I have found them to be a lot like me, and now I can relate to them better.

The psalmist said, **"When I kept silent, (living in denial?) my bones were wasting away with groans, day in and day out; day and night Your hand lay heavy on me. At last, I admitted to You I had sinned, no longer concealing my guilt, I said, I will go to the Lord and confess my fault. And You, Lord, You have forgiven the wrong I did and have pardoned my sin"** (based on Ps. 32).

After Joe admitted his perfectionism, he went through the next phase of the surrender cycle, the struggle to believe that his "diagnosis" was right. He began to rationalize: "Okay, so maybe I am a perfectionist, but it's really not so bad after all. I mean, who is hurt by my perfectionism? I could have worse problems, like alcoholism or drug addiction."

Joe's family was on the edge of breaking up. He was taking medication for high blood pressure. He was frantic about his future. He had few good friendships. All of these were clear indications that something was wrong with his lifestyle. Admitting to this was really hard for Joe. He wavered in his admission until he was thoroughly convinced that his compulsion would ultimately destroy him.

The struggle phase is perhaps the most difficult. Denial is a tremendous force that wants to keep us blinded and in bondage. The struggle to be honest and stay honest takes, to begin with, concentrated effort. With practice, this phase gets easier.

At this point, Joe moved into the surrender phase. Surrender is letting go; accepting who you are; coming to God and saying, "Lord, this is who I really am. This is the real me. I've had it. I'm fed up with the way I am. I need Your help, Lord Jesus."

Surrender means turning over to Jesus all that we discover about ourselves. It does not mean we give up and give in to our compulsions, problems, struggles, and issues. It means we turn them over, one by one, as they are brought forward in our lives, and we graciously let Jesus do what needs to be done, in His way and in His own good time.

We are told by the author of Hebrews to keep our eyes fixed on Jesus. Paul tells us in Colossians 3:1–3 to let our thoughts be on heavenly things, to look to Christ who is sitting at God's right hand.

The result and the final phase of this cycle is serenity. This fifth phase is a by-product that comes as we become aware of, admit, struggle through, and surrender our issues to the Lord.

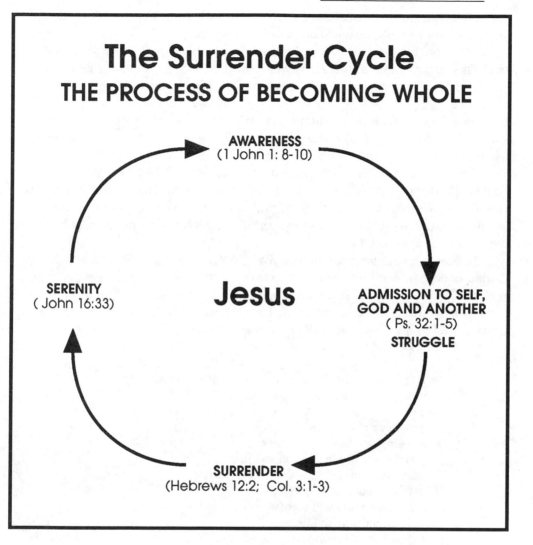

The Surrender Cycle
THE PROCESS OF BECOMING WHOLE

AWARENESS
(1 John 1: 8-10)

ADMISSION TO SELF,
GOD AND ANOTHER
(Ps. 32:1-5)

STRUGGLE

Jesus

SERENITY
(John 16:33)

SURRENDER
(Hebrews 12:2; Col. 3:1-3)

Many make the mistake of seeking serenity at all costs. This becomes the goal in their lives. They are often prey to the New Age movement and other ''quick-fix'' ideas. Lasting peace and serenity come through going through all phases of the process and focusing clearly on Jesus Christ all along the way.

The more I have practiced using this cycle, the more serenity I have been given. This approach to life is now second nature to me—in major issues as well as minor difficulties.

Step One asks us to admit that we are powerless over certain parts of our lives. It asks us to admit our need for God's help. We simply cannot change some situations, no matter how much effort we put into them.

Step Two acknowledges that although we may be powerless, Jesus Christ is not. This step reminds us that He is with us and can change our weaknesses into strengths. It asks that we "come to believe" in His power to change what we cannot change.

Step Three urges us to entrust our wills and lives to Him. It asks us to surrender to our Creator all that we have and all that we are. It is an action step, asking us to "turn" ourselves over to Jesus.

For some people this is a difficult step. Some may feel that they need to "make it" alone in life, that they need to be self-sufficient. Others may feel that it is a sign of weakness to ask for help. Still others believe that surrender implies giving up. And many think that every part of their lives must be in order before they can even approach God.

In Step Three, surrender means giving my will and my life over to Jesus Christ, each day, each moment, just the way that I am. It is synonymous with seeking His presence, guidance, and counsel throughout the day. Surrender leads to serenity. After I have surrendered, I have peace and serenity. The Serenity Prayer, brief as it is, best captures the surrender cycle.

> God,
> grant me the serenity to accept the things I cannot change,
> courage to change the things I can
> and wisdom to know the difference,
> living one day at a time,
> enjoying one moment at a time,
> accepting hardship as a pathway to peace,
> taking as Jesus did, this sinful world as it is,
> not as I would have it,
> trusting that You will make all things right
> as I surrender to Your will,
> so that I may be reasonably happy in this life
> and supremely happy with You forever in the next.[1]

Please indicate the appropriate responses below:

1. Initially, this is my reaction to the Third Step:
____ It confuses me. I'm still not sure what this all means.

---

[1]The first three lines of this prayer are most commonly used in A.A. circles. The prayer in its entirety has been attributed to Reinhold Niebuhr.

___ It makes me a little scared. I don't know what will happen next.

___ It makes me eager for more.

___ I want to wait and see and hear more before I say or do anything.

___ I have turned my will and life over to Jesus Christ to the best of my knowledge and ability.

2. List below the names of all the people you know who have been hurt, harmed, or disappointed by Jesus when they have turned their lives over to Him.

_____

3. Indicate where you are with this step:

___ I didn't know that Jesus wants my life.

___ I have given Him my will.

___ I have given Him my life.

___ I don't understand how to do this.

___ I'm interested but scared.

___ I don't know where I am with this step.

4. When I think of turning my will and life over to Jesus Christ, I feel (for instance, relief, fear, excitement)

_____

_____

5. Jesus says, **"I am standing at your door knocking. If one of you hears Me calling and opens the door, I will come in to share your meal, side by side with you"** (based on Revelation 3:20).

As best I can determine, what is holding me back from turning my will and life over to Jesus Christ right now is (my pride—I want to do life my own way.):

_____

_____

_____

6. When I think of Jesus as *my* Savior, I recognize that He has saved me *from* (workaholism, perfectionism, fear, ultimately from death):

_____

_____

_____

7. When I think of Jesus as *my* Savior, I recognize that he has saved me *for* (serving others in speaking and writing):

_____

_____

_____

8. At this point, the one obstacle that seems to prevent me from entrusting my life to Jesus Christ is

____ my idol (_____). It/he/she, is what I think about most each day.

____ my fantasy (_____). It controls me.

____ my false god (_____). It's the person/thing I worship the most each day.

____ my "toys" (_____).

____ my stubbornness. I want to control my life.

_____

_____

_____

Who is in control of your life right now? To what or whom have you given permission to be the god of your life at this present moment?

I admit that the god of my life is often "ideal-aholism." I am an ideal-aholic. That means I am driven by the ideal. I think everything should be ideal, wonderful, and perfect. I assume all movies and life stories should have a happy ending. This is another expression of "god-playing"—that is, I want things to go my way or the way I think they should go.

When I am getting tense or anxious, it sometimes means I am trying to control my situation. When this happens, physical symptoms begin to emerge. I realize that ideal-aholism is kicking in and that I'm trying to impose my standard on my situation. I am trying to control things so that everyone will be "ideally" happy. When I admit to myself what I am doing, the neck ache, pain in my back, or rumbling stomach generally disappears.

This is a frequent battle with me. It is a battle for lordship. Am I my own god? Do I create my own destiny? Or do I let God be God and let Him do things His way?

Some say our god is whatever we think about most. Do you believe that? If so, what/who is your god today?

Check the things below that seem to be the gods in your life:

___ TV	___ Drugs
___ The office	___ Movies
___ A friend	___ Laziness
___ Excitement	___ Fantasies
___ Sex	___ Alcohol
___ Soda	___ Myself
___ Chocolate	___ An affair
___ Food	___ Stability/security
___ Smoking	___ Money/material things
___ Sports	___ Cars
___ Houses/property	___ Upward mobility
___ Clothes	___ Shopping
___ I just gotta have all the latest "toys" and gimmicks	

___ _____   ___ _____

___ _____   ___ _____

"I remember when I was in high school," my good friend Sue told me, "I suffered a real identity crisis, feeling two separate personalities struggling for control inside my imperfect body. On Saturday night I was a girlfriend to a guy in a letter jacket, 'in love' with him and with my lifestyle, and on Sunday morning I belonged to my Lord and Savior.

"The problem was I wasn't really ready to call Him Lord, at least not for the whole weekend. My guilt was real and plenty strong, but the attachment to the world was stronger.

"In college it didn't get any better. In fact, as I matured through four years of college and my first full-time job and early married years, more and more things seemed to be taken away from His lordship. Worship was important, but not the most important Sunday priority, and money was spent before I had a chance to count it. Marriage was a challenge at best. I was frustrated, disappointed, and often downright angry. What could it have been about this unsatisfactory, burdensome lifestyle that I was afraid of losing?

"When I was about thirty, I became involved in a neighborhood Bible study and bridged the gap between giving for myself and giving of myself. The deeper I dug, the higher I climbed, and so many of the other areas of my life began to come together. In responding to the invitation to turn over the frustrations, desires, self-centered temper displays, and boredom to the One who knows me best, I honestly discovered a direction for my life that had been there all along, hidden deep within the person I thought I should be.

"I still forget to do it. But every time I remember to surrender my circumstances and attitude into the keeping of a faithful God, the things I can't control or ever face are erased from my mind, and I'm back on track, thankful and filled with hope and purpose.''

What the Bible Says about Step Three

I turn my will and my life over to Jesus Christ, my Lord and Savior.

Choose one passage from the selections given and read it each day during the next week. Think about the passage by checking the statements below that reflect how you feel. Then write your own personal application of the passage as a final comment.

Now that we've looked more closely at who Jesus is, let's look at the invitation He gave to each of us.

1. Matthew 11:28–30: After teaching His disciples about their mission, He spoke to all the people who would listen, and extended this invitation: **"Come to Me, all you who labor and are heavy laden, and I will give you rest. Take My yoke upon you and learn from Me, for I am gentle and lowly in heart, and you will find rest for your souls. For My yoke is easy and My burden is light."**

____ This is me. I'm tired. I'm ready to give my life over to Jesus Christ.

____ I want to know more about what Jesus' yoke would be like for me.

____ _____

____ _____

____ _____

2. John 1:12: As he describes Jesus coming to us as a human being, John realistically lets us know that some people would not accept Jesus: **"But as many as received Him, to them He gave the right to become children of God."**

____ At times in my life I have rejected Jesus Christ.

____ Since I have received Jesus Christ into my life, I have been given the power to be one of His children.

____ I would like to learn more about what it means to be a child of God.

____ _____

____ _____

____ _____

3. 2 Corinthians 5:17–21: Paul describes what happens to the person who says yes to Jesus and receives Him. Paul says, **"Therefore, if anyone is in Christ, he is a new creation; old things have passed away; behold, all things have become new"** (v. 17).

_____ I know this is true for me. I am in a relationship with Jesus Christ. I am a new creation.

_____ I am struggling like crazy with my old life.

_____ _____

_____ _____

_____ _____

4. Galatians 2:20: Our faith in Jesus Christ is what saves us, Paul says. No one can be justified by keeping the Law. My justification has taken place already because **"I have been crucified with Christ; it is no longer I who live, but Christ lives in me; and the life which I now live in the flesh I live by faith in the Son of God, who loved me and gave Himself for me."**

_____ This passage is true for me. This is my experience.

_____ I don't have to "play god." Jesus is my God. My old self has been crucified with Him. I can now live a life of faith pleasing to Him.

_____ _____

_____ _____

_____ _____

Taking Step Three is a choice that we make freely and deliberately. It is a choice that we make in stages. The more we get to know Jesus, the more we trust Him and give Him more of ourselves. Although this Step may feel a bit scary, there's really nothing to be afraid of. Jesus Christ is the kindest, most gentle, and most loving person history has ever known. He can be trusted.

Step Three is important because so much is at stake. You may decide not to turn your will and life over to Jesus. That means you have decided that you will continue to be your own savior.

God loves you. He does have a plan for you. His plan is rich and full of life. When we turn ourselves over to our Creator, our lives are fulfilling. If we hold back, we may be missing out on the great things God has in store for us.

Ask Him to make Himself and His plan known to you. Your life will become more directed, and you will become more like Him. When you turn your will and life over to Jesus, you will know peace.

A Surrender Prayer

Dear Lord Jesus Christ,

You truly are my Lord and I am Your servant.

I am sorry that I so often get those two roles turned around. I want with all my heart to turn my will and my life over to You. I know that I am unworthy of Your love, but I also know that You know me and You came for people like me.

I am one of those ''independent spirits'' who wants to do life my way. Please help me to let this go so that I can do life Your way. I want to be in a relationship with You.

Jesus, I'm afraid to give You my life. I've fought so long and hard to keep it. Just when I feel like I have it, I feel this tug inside to turn it back over to You. I know it would be best for me. Sometimes I feel so close. Please help me to surrender all of myself.

I want, Lord to love You more than anything else. You have given me so much, Lord. Please grant me this one more request so that I may better serve You and others.

Being born from above is the same, I believe, as turning your will and life over to Jesus Christ. By turning our lives over to Jesus Christ moment by moment, we can gradually learn how to live a new style of life—a life that is truly Christ-centered, not self-centered, a style of life that is fun, adventurous, and free.

Doing Step Three

''I turn my will and my life over to Jesus Christ, my Lord and Savior.''

Step Three, turning our lives over to Jesus, is a hard step. God has given us freedom, freedom to choose. This step, in one sense, asks us to give that freedom back to God. It asks us to give control of our lives back to Him. To surrender. To let go. To let God work in and through us. To let Him be Lord.

This step asks us to trust. Specifically, it asks us to trust Jesus Christ. This Step asks us to give Him our wills and our lives. Our wills are our decision-making abilities. Our lives are everything else: feelings, friends, possessions, problems, ideas, dreams, pain, and this moment. In other words, *everything*. What He gives us in return is *everything*.

To do so, we must first know Jesus, for none of us can trust someone we do not know. Who is this Jesus?

Those who knew Jesus best—His disciples, Matthew, Mark, Luke, and

John—describe Him to us in the first four books of the New Testament. Let's look at a few passages that show Him as He really is.

Check the boxes of the passages you have read. Write a summary of each passage and what it means to you.

• Jesus is the Great Healer. He said, **"It is not the healthy who need a doctor, but the sick. I did not come to call the fit and the flourishing, but the sinners"** (based on Mark 2:17). (For instance, Jesus came for me. I'm not perfect. I'm a sinner. I admit I need Jesus to heal me.)

_____

_____

_____

• Jesus defends the weak and accepts all people. As Jesus was teaching the people, the religious leaders brought a woman who had been caught committing adultery. They made her stand in full view of everybody and said to Jesus, "Master, this woman was caught in the very act of committing adultery, and Moses ordered us in the Law to condemn women like this to death by stoning. What do you have to say? Do we stone her or strangle her?"

These religious leaders were testing Him, looking for something to use against Him. But Jesus bent down and started writing on the ground with His finger. As they persisted, He looked up and said, "If there is one of you who has not sinned, let him be the first to throw a stone at her." Then he bent down and wrote on the ground again.

When they heard this, they went away, one by one, beginning with the eldest, until Jesus was left alone with the woman, who remained standing there. He looked up and said to her, "Woman, where are they? Has no one condemned you?"

"No one, sir," she replied.

"Neither do I condemn you," said Jesus. **"Go away and don't sin anymore"** (based on John 8:1–11).

Write down your feelings in response to the scene described here (I feel accepted by Jesus. Scenes like this one help me to feel Jesus' compassion):

_____

_____

_____

• Jesus is the Good Shepherd who has come to bring me a full life. He said, **"My sheep hear My voice....I call them one by one and lead them. I will go ahead of My sheep; they will follow Me because they know My voice.**

"I am the gate. Anyone who enters through Me will be safe....I have come to bring you life, an abundant life....I am the Good Shepherd: the good shepherd is one who lays down his life for his sheep. I know My own sheep and My own know Me. And I lay down My life for My sheep" (based on John 10:1–16). (Jesus is my Good Shepherd. I listen for His voice. I know that He is there to guide me and protect me.)

_____

_____

_____

• Jesus is the Son of God
    John says:

> **Jesus was there from the very beginning.**
> **Through Him all things were created,**
>   **not one thing had its being except through Him.**
> **All that came to be had life in Him**
> **and that life was the light of men,**
> **a light that shines in the dark,**
> **a light that darkness could not overpower.**
> **God became flesh and lived among us** (based on John 1:1–14).

Write your response to this passage (You are my creator, Lord Jesus. You are the light that shines into the darkness in my world. I give You thanks today):

_____

_____

_____

Making Step Three My Own

This section provides you with a format for integrating your feelings, responses to questions, and what you learned from this step, the Scriptures, and your group meetings.

Date, day, and time of your writings:

_____

1. At this point in my life, the major area that I am working on (for instance, identifying the ways in which I play god each day):

_____

_____

2. Major insights I was given into my life through this step (I have been given the privilege of choice. I can turn my life over to God or I can try to run it by myself.):

_____

_____

_____

_____

3. The scriptural passage that spoke to me most clearly in this step (I have been crucified with Christ—Gal 2:20.):

_____

The one word that has been most important to me in this chapter (Control—I often seek to control my life and the life of others.):

_____

_____

4. The major discovery about Jesus Christ that I was given in this step (He wants me to give Him my life.):

_____

_____

5. The strongest feeling I have as I have worked this step (Relief—it is good to surrender to God.):

_____

6. The action I feel called to take as a result of working this step (I plan to let go more and let God do what needs to be done.):

_____

7. The good news for me in this step and these passages (When I let go, God can take over.):

_____

CHAPTER 4

KNOW YOURSELF TO LOVE YOURSELF

▼

Step Four:

I begin honestly listing

what I know and discover

about myself: my strengths,

weaknesses, and behavior.

My life is a blank. I feel so empty and lonely. I don't know what value my life has for me or anyone else. I just want to give up." These are the words of Sam, a person I had been working with for several weeks.

He was discovering that his identity had been wrapped up in pleasing others. He was so intent on making others happy, especially those in his family, that he had no idea what he himself wanted out of life.

When I asked him what he enjoyed doing on a day off, "I don't know" was the best response he could come up with. His days off always revolved around what others wanted to do.

Sam knew that he needed to discover himself. "Since I've been in the second grade, I've been lost. I lost myself back there somewhere, and I don't know who I am," he said. He wanted more than anything to know himself and let others know who he is.

This fourth step was crucial for him as he sought to be healthy. It is a crucial step for *anyone* who wants to be healthy. We cannot love what we do not know. Do we love ourselves as we are? Have we been deceiving ourselves about who we really are?

Serving on a state pardon board for eleven years, I heard the stories of hundreds of prison inmates trying to convince our five-member board that they should be released. Many of them had lied to themselves for so long that they were convinced they were not guilty of the crimes they had committed and been convicted of. So they had the courage to try to persuade the Pardon Board that their sentences should be reduced or they should be released.

The truth always did come out through court reports, their own testimony, witnesses, parole officers, and penitentiary officials. Justice was done in almost all cases.

We, too, are criminals. "The difference between you and me," one angry prison inmate told me, "is that you folks on the outside do what we did, but you haven't been caught yet."

All of us can easily and subtly deceive ourselves. Our real personalities and our real motives can get buried and lost. It takes a deliberate choice and continuous work to keep in touch with our real selves.

What about You?

When I see a floral arrangement, one of the first questions that passes through my mind is, *Are these real flowers or are they silk?* The imitation flowers are done so beautifully that it's sometimes hard to distinguish them from genuine flowers.

Do we know and love our real selves, or do we know and love an imitation of ourselves? Who are we? Who am I? What have I become? What is my lifestyle doing to me? Am I losing touch with my own soul?

We are commanded by Jesus to love our neighbors as we love ourselves. It's no wonder we love our neighbors so poorly. It has little to do with our neighbors and a great deal to do with us.

The following pages will help you do a fourth-step inventory. No one expects you to complete these pages quickly. Take your time. Glance over them each week and add to the lists you've begun. Set a goal for yourself, a realistic goal for a tentative completion date. Then if you feel you still need time, extend the date. Some people have spent years working on this step. The Bible gives us a good beginning point.

What the Bible Says about Step Four

Jesus had an important conversation with a woman who discovered herself in the process. He reminded her of some things she had forgotten. She had chosen to forget some things that His simple presence brought to her mind.

He had left Judea and gone back to Galilee. This meant that He had to cross Samaria, a country that was not favorably inclined toward Jews. On the way He came to the Samaritan town called Sychar, near the land that Jacob gave to his son Joseph. Jacob's well is there, and Jesus, tired from the journey, sat down by the well. It was about noon. His disciples had gone into the town to buy lunch. When a Samaritan woman came to draw water, Jesus said to her, "Give Me a drink."

The Samaritan woman said to Him, "What? You are a Jew and You ask me, a Samaritan woman, for a drink? Jews don't associate with Samaritans."

Jesus replied, ''If you only knew what God is offering and Who it is that is saying to you: give Me a drink, you would have been the one to ask and He would have given you living water.''

''You have no bucket, Sir,'' she answered, ''and the well is deep: how could You get this living water? Are You a greater man than our father Jacob who gave us this well?''

''Whoever drinks this water will get thirsty again; but anyone who drinks the water that I give will never be thirsty again; the water that I give will turn into a spring inside him, welling up to eternal life.''

''Sir,'' said the woman ''give me some of that water so that I will never get thirsty and never have to come here again to get water.''

''Go and call your husband,'' Jesus said to her, ''and come back here.''

The woman answered, ''I have no husband.''

He said to her, ''You are right to say, 'I have no husband,' for although you have had five, the one you have now is not your husband. You spoke the truth there.''

''I see you are some kind of prophet, Sir,'' said the woman. ''I know that Messiah, the Christ, is coming; and when He comes He will tell us everything.''

''I who am speaking to you,'' said Jesus, ''I am He.''

The woman put down her water jar and hurried back to the town to tell the people, ''Come and see a man who has told me everything I ever did; I wonder if he is the Christ.'' This brought people out of the town, and they started walking towards Him.

Many Samaritans of that town had believed in Him on the strength of the woman's testimony when she said, ''He told me all I have ever done'' (based on John 4:1–26).

Please answer the questions below; then proceed through pages 70 through 71, writing down the first things that come to your mind in each category. It could be that's all the work you'll need to do on this step. Later, perhaps a few days from your initial exposure to these pages, look at your comments and add to them if you wish.

1. What impresses me most about this true story is:
____ That Jesus goes to a foreign territory (Samaria) to reach out.
____ That Jesus is not bound by the cultural mores of the day.
____ That Jesus expresses a need (for water).
____ The promise that Jesus gives to the woman.
____ The fact that Jesus reveals who He is.
____ Jesus' approach to the woman.

2. As far as I'm concerned, this story is about
____ The relationship of the Jews with the Samaritans.
____ Water.
____ Women.
____ Jesus knowing everything about us.
____ Cultural norms.
____ All of the above.

3. If I had been the woman at the well and Jesus had told me that He knew all about my personal life, I would have:
____ Run scared.
____ Bowed down in fear.
____ Been embarrassed.
____ Been relieved—finally someone knows the real me.
____ Been silenced.

4. When I remember that God does know me as I am,
____ I feel free to be myself.
____ I worry less.
____ I worry more.
____ I feel anxious.
____ I avoid thinking about this.

5. Jesus' promise, **"The water that I give will become in you a fountain of water springing up to eternal life,"** makes me
____ Wonder about the meaning of all this.
____ Feel great—I have experienced this fountain of water within me.
____ Express gratitude.
____ Feel left out—I don't feel I have this.
____ Want to know more—I want this fountain flowing inside me.
____ Grateful for Jesus Christ.

The psalmist says, **"I am wonderful...and my soul knows this very well"** (based on Ps. 139:14). Many of the people I work with don't believe this. They have become separated from their souls. They have lost their hearts and their hearts' desire. They don't know what they want anymore.

Some of these friends can no longer hear the messages God has to give to us—

- That we are loved by him
- That we are gifted
- That we are precious
- That we are a work of art (just as we are)

We are too busy, too active and too consumed with everyday life. (Maybe a prison term would be a gift for some of us!). These important messages cannot get through to us. And then we fret. We wonder about our own value and significance. We begin to do all that society tells us to do to feel important. As we seek the approval of others, we lose the sense of approval God has given us. We forget to listen to His words first. We lose ourselves in the standards that others give to us.

When our children were born they could do only two things: (1) cry; and (2) soil their diapers. (They were really good at this second one.) At that age, they could do nothing to impress us or give love to us. All they could do was *be*. Their *be*ing was what we loved. That is what we still love about them. Nothing will change that love.

That is how God feels about us today. When we believe this, then we are courageous enough to honestly look at this fourth step.

Doing Step Four

I begin honestly listing what I know and discover about myself: my strengths, weaknesses, and behavior.

The Fourth-Step Inventory

"A well-defined person is a mature person," a therapist friend of mine told me recently. "Healthy people know their own boundaries, talents, and capabilities and then use all these to live more fulfilling lives."

The fourth step calls us back. It challenges us to come back to our own core and soul. It asks us to reflect. It invites us to take inventory by looking at four dimensions of our lives:

1. Where did I come from?
2. Who am I right now?
3. What have I been given?
4. And what am I doing with what I have been given?

Each time you complete a part of this inventory, begin with a prayer like this one.

A Fourth-Step Prayer

Dear Lord Jesus,

I don't want to kid myself. I want to know who I really am. Even though I am afraid of this sometimes, I really do want to know myself better. I know I have strengths and weaknesses. That's the way my life is now. I'm sure that's the way it will always be. Help me to be okay with that.

Help me to believe that You love me as I am. Help me to love myself as I am. Help me to love others as they are.

Please give me an understanding of my gifts and talents so that I may properly use them to have a full life and help others in the process.

Thank You, Lord Jesus.

1. Where Did I Come From?

My feelings about my home, schools, teachers, and classmates (one-sentence descriptions of the first thing that comes to mind)

Ages 1-5 (For instance, I felt loved and wanted.):

_____

_____

Ages 6-9 (This period of my life is kind of a blank.):

_____

_____

Ages 10-12 (I have good feelings about my uncle who spent a lot of time with me during these years.):

_____

_____

Junior High School (I remember feelings of fear, loneliness, turmoil, self-consciousness.):

_____

_____

Senior High School (I remember searching and being unsettled. I'll never forget my first girlfriend.):

_____

_____

College (fun, adventure, hopefulness):

_____

_____

My first job (feeling insecure, afraid of the future, like it was my "god"):

_____

_____

My profession (a struggle; hopeful; fulfillment—I'm persistent):

_____

_____

Some of the people/things that helped make me the way I am now (My grandparents were always there for me when I came home from school. They listened to me as I described my day.). Write about your father, mother, siblings, spouse, children, and other influential family members:

_____

_____

_____

_____

_____

_____

_____

_____

_____

_____

_____

_____

_____

Other important information about who I am now (I feel I am moving closer to what God has given me to do; I can relax more; I have learned a great deal about my own needs.):

_____

_____

_____

_____

_____

_____

_____

_____

There are many other tools available to help you get to know yourself better. Some test examples include Myers-Briggs, DISC, Hoyt-Wagner Gifts Study, and Taylor-Johnson. The best resource is within you—the Holy Spirit. He will lead you and guide you into all truth. Using the Scriptures as your guide, let God teach you about who you are and where you are in life.

2. Who Am I Right Now?

How do I feel about myself right now (check one or several)?
_____ I feel loved as I am.
_____ I feel I'm a good person.
_____ I feel like I am a bad person.
_____ I feel I need to do things faster than others to be loved.
_____ I feel I need to be perfect to be loved.

What do I really like (tennis, Chinese food, dogs, children)?

_____

_____

_____

_____

What do I really dislike (cats, my overreaction to people who disagree with me, overdrafts)? _____

_____

_____

_____

_____

What encourages me most (hugs from members of my family, a phone call from my best friend)? _____

_____

_____

_____

What discourages me most (my judgmentalism, financial problems)? _____

_____

_____

My strengths (my health, my positive attitude, my ability to do a variety of things well): _____

_____

_____

_____

My weaknesses (I am too idealistic; I cannot do accounting; I am not a good administrator.):

_____

_____

_____

Some things I like about my body (I am capable of working out; I like my weight; I feel attractive.): _____

_____

_____

_____

_____

Some things I like about my mind and the way I think (I can think on my feet; I am quick.): _____

_____

_____

_____

Some things I like about my personality (I like to reach out to touch others; I like how friendly I can be.): _____

_____

_____

_____

Some things that I can really do well (ski, racquetball, swim, talk to strangers, give presentations): _____

_____

_____

_____

A few things I know I'm _not_ good at (supervising others, major construction projects): _____

_____

_____

_____

What I feel I want to do with my life in the future (keep doing what I'm doing, change my career, plan for retirement):

_____

_____

_____

_____

_____

3. What Have I Been Given?

We have all been given the gift of life. Listed below are passages that describe other specific gifts that have been given to us. Quickly glance through this list and especially notice the italicized words that describe what we have been given.

> **If anyone is in Christ, that person is a *new creation*. The old has passed away and the new has come** (based on 2 Cor. 5:17).
>
> **God loved the world so much that He gave His only Son so that everyone who believes in Him will not be lost but have *eternal life*** (based on John 3:16).
>
> **If you make my word your home, you will indeed be My disciples, you will learn the truth and the *truth will make you free*. If the Son sets you free, you will be free indeed** (based on John 8:32, 35).
>
> **There is *no condemnation* for those who are in Christ Jesus** (based on Rom. 8:1).
>
> **Blessed be the God and Father of our Lord Jesus Christ who has *blessed us with all the spiritual blessings of heaven* in Christ. Before the world was made, He *chose us* in Christ, to be *holy and spotless* and to *live in His presence*. We have become His *adopted* sons and daughters, chosen from the beginning, through Jesus Christ, *for His own kind purposes*. He gives us *freedom* and the *forgiveness* of our sins. He has *let us know the mystery* of His purpose . . . that He will bring everything together under Christ. *We have heard* the message of the truth and the good news of our salvation and *have believed* it. We have been given the faith to *put our hope in Christ* and we have been *stamped with the seal of the Holy Spirit*** (based on Eph. 1:3–14).

You Are Gifted

Paul tells us that each person is given a *gift for the good of all* (based on 1 Cor. 12:7). Please read through the list of spiritual gifts below. Indicate which of these gifts you know you have been given. Put a question mark by those that you think you might have but are not certain of. If you have questions or would like to do further study on this subject, please refer to *Mastering Life* (Prince of Peace Publishing, 200 East Nicollet Boulevard, Burnsville, MN 55337) or use the Hoyt-Modified Wagner Spiritual Gifts assessment form (available from Fuller Seminary, P.O. Box 91990, Pasadena, CA 91109).

____ The gift of God's love
____ The gift of Jesus Christ
____ The gift of eternal life
____ The gift of the Bible
____ The gift of gathering with other believers
____ The gift of the Holy Spirit
____ The gift of the fruits of the Holy Spirit
____ The gift of being a founding leader/apostle
____ The gift of being a prophet
____ The gift of telling others about God
____ The gift of being a pastor
____ The gift of being a teacher
____ The gift of wisdom
____ The gift of knowledge
____ The gift of faith
____ The gift of healing
____ The gift of miraculous powers
____ The gift of discernment
____ The gift of speaking/praying in an unknown "prayer language" (tongues)
____ The gift of helping others
____ The gift of administration
____ The gift of ministering to others
____ The gift of preaching
____ The gift of exhortation
____ The gift of alms-giving
____ The gift of mercy

As part of your prayer and mediation time this week, read the following paraphrases:

You, Oh God, created every part of me. You put me together in my mother's womb. I praise You because You are to be feared. Everything You do is strange and wonderful. I know it with all my heart.

When my bones were being formed and carefully put together in my mother's womb, when I was growing there in secret, You knew I was there; You saw me before I was born. The days given to me had all been recorded in Your book before any of them ever began (based on Ps. 139:13–16).

We are God's work of art, created in Jesus Christ (based on Eph. 2:10).

4. What Am I Doing with What I Have Been Given?

Am I using my gifts?

      ____ yes   ____ no

Am I working on my weaknesses?

      ____ yes   ____ no

List them (letting go, not doing everything perfectly, getting more organized, moving beyond procrastination, facing my issues):

_____

_____

Parts of my life that are sinful and need forgiveness (such as my judgmentalism, my lack of trust in God, worrying, my resentful thoughts, my criticism of others):

_____

_____

What I am doing that I should not be doing (working in the wrong job, going to movies that influence me negatively, stuffing my feelings rather than sharing them openly with my spouse):

_____

_____

_____

What I am not doing that I should be doing (spending more time in prayer each day, writing more, calling my friends more often, using my gift of teaching more consistently):

_____

_____

_____

What I am addicted to right now (TV, sexual fantasies, food):

_____

_____

_____

The following are specific sins that I need forgiveness for (not using the gifts and talents I have been given, lusting, being critical):

_____

_____

_____

I know that the following patterns of behavior are operative in my life (I know that I judge people. Because I do, some of them don't get close to me. I want to accept people as they are, not judge them.):

_____

_____

_____

Listed below are the times/experiences/incidents when I did not trust God. (Last week when a big project fell through; I see good coming from that now, but then I didn't trust. I was upset instead.)

_____

_____

_____

Listed below are my "idols," "lords," and "false gods" today (success, my life plan, my desire to have more security, money):

_____

_____

_____

_____

Making Step Four My Own

This section provides you with a format for integrating your feelings, responses to questions, and what you learned from this step, the Scriptures, and your group meetings.

Date, day, and time of your writings:

_____

1. At this point in my life, the major area that I am working on is (for instance, getting to know myself better by spending time once each week to reflect on who I am and then making notes in this book):

_____

_____

2. Major insights I was given into my life through this step (how important it is for me to know my weaknesses and not be afraid to face them):

_____

_____

_____

_____

3. The scriptural passage that spoke to me most clearly in this step (I am wonderful and my soul knows this very well. Most of the time I don't believe this.):

_____

The one word that has been most important to me in this chapter (Honesty—I begin honestly listing . . .):

_____

_____

4. The major discovery about Jesus Christ that I was given in this step (Jesus has set me free. I can be myself.):

_____

_____

5. The strongest feeling I have as I have worked this step (the joy of re-discovering parts of myself—gifts I had forgotten I have):

_____

6. The action I feel called to take as a result of working this step (I will spend time each week thinking about who I am and adding my discoveries to the lists I began in Step Four.):

_____

7. The good news for me in this step and these passages (I am lovable as I am.):

_____

CHAPTER 5

FREE AT
LAST

▼

Step Five:

I am ready to honestly share

with God and another

person the exact nature of

my strengths, weaknesses,

and behavior.

friend in ministry told me recently he is convinced that most adults want two major things to happen in their lifetime: (1) They want to be known for who they really are; (2) they want to know another for who that person really is.

Do you think this is true? Is this the way it is for you?

Step Five gives me permission to honestly share the real me with God and another person. This means I am willing to let the other person see my strengths as well as my weaknesses. I allow God and that other person(s) to know my behavior, without defending or explaining it. This can be an extremely difficult step to get started with. We all want this, yet we are all afraid of it.

Step Five can be the most freeing of all the steps. God wants us to be free and whole. Secrets, schizophrenic behavior, denial, partial truths, and unresolved "business" from our past keep us in bondage and slavery. Sin or a secret activity will keep us in darkness. God wants us to be free, to live in the light. Jesus came to bring us freedom.

One of the pathways to that freedom, I believe, is to have a sincere conversation with Jesus. A suggestion would be to take the written work you did in your fourth-step inventory and bring it to the Lord. This could be an extended time while on a long walk or a long visit in a chapel. Maybe a weekend at a retreat center would work for you. It could be a time of extended conversation with Jesus about who you are and what you have done. He is faithful; He will forgive us. He is there to affirm us. He will guide us into the future.

It may be time, too, to do the same with a close friend or pastor. We are all aware of the need to do "spring cleaning" in our homes. The same must be done in our souls. By making an "appointment" with that person, we are doing "spring cleaning" in our lives.

Years ago, Catholics had an exercise called General Confession. At several intervals in life, a person was asked to "review" his or her life up to that point.

After doing this "assessment," the person was to go to a priest and share his/her "life story."

There were several reasons for this General Confession:

1. It gave the person permission to check out how he or she was doing in his or her relationship with God and others.
2. It gave the person the platform to share what he or she had discovered with another person.
3. It helped the person see his or her need for Jesus Christ and His forgiveness.
4. It gave the person some feedback about his or her lifestyle. It encouraged him or her and affirmed his or her humanness.
5. It gave the person an opportunity to confess to God and another person the unconfessed sins of the past. It gave that person the hope of a new beginning.

I think this General Confession was a great practice. It has long been lost in the shuffle. Step Five brings the concept back in a new way. It provides a way for all of us to experience the freedom and joy in being honest with ourselves, God, and another person.

I have learned that my best friends are those who know me best. They know my strengths, my weaknesses, and all the peculiar characteristics of my behavior.

All of us have the same basic relational desires. We all seek to have at least one deep long-term friendship. We all seek to have someone who knows us as we really are; even if we are afraid of this, we know deep down that we want to be known. We all seek to know at least one other person as that person really is. If these desires are not satisfied, life can be lonely.

Shirley had known about the steps for years. She was afraid of doing the fourth and fifth steps. It took her seven years to get up enough courage to begin Step Four and then another year before she could actually go to someone and do Step Five.

"At first I didn't think it was right to go to anyone with this information about myself," she said. "*Why would anyone want to listen to my story?* I had often thought to myself. But then I realized it wasn't my responsibility to be concerned about them. I needed to go and get this stuff out of my system so that I could become a healthy person.

"It's the best thing I've ever done for myself. I feel liberated in knowing that at least one other person knows me and accepts me for who I am."

What the Bible Says about Step Five

I am ready to honestly share with God and another person the exact nature of my strengths, weaknesses and behavior.

Before you talk to another person about your Step Four inventory, think about the truth of the Scriptures below:

1. Jesus was confronted by the Pharisees for eating with tax collectors and sinners. In response to their challenge, Jesus said, **"Those who are well have no need of a physician, but those who are sick. I did not come to call the righteous, but sinners, to repentance"** (Mark 2:17).

Choose from the following:
____ I have always known this is true, but never believed it.
____ This is hard to believe, really.
____ Jesus came for me. I know I am a sinner. I need Him.
____ This amazes me. Why would Jesus come for sinners or the unhealthy?

2. In his first letter, John writes to the early Christians to lay out the cards: **If we say we have no sin in us, we are deceiving ourselves and refusing to admit the truth; but if we admit to our sins, then God who is faithful and just will forgive us our sins ... but to say that we have never sinned is to call God a liar** (based on 1 John 1:8–10).

Choose from the following:
____ I know I am a sinner, but I don't admit it.
____ I admit I am a sinner in a general sense. I don't think of specific sins when I confess my sins in church or at home.
____ I don't know what sin is.

3. In His conversation with Nicodemus, a leading Jew who came to see Jesus at night, Jesus set the record straight about who He was and what His purpose in coming was: **"For God did not send His Son into the world to condemn the world, but that the world through Him might be saved"** (John 3:17).
____ God has sent Jesus to save me, not condemn me. I now believe this is the truth regardless of how I have previously thought about Him.
____ I want to confess my sins and be forgiven.
____ I often feel condemned. This passage is good news for me. I want to believe that Jesus came to save me.

4. The psalmist was a great psychologist. His advice was clear and practical—don't stuff your feelings or your sin:

> **Blessed is he whose transgressions are forgiven, whose sins are covered. Blessed is the man whose sin the LORD does not count against him and in whose spirit is no deceit. When I kept silent, my bones wasted away through my groaning all day long. For day and night Your hand was heavy upon me; my strength was sapped as in the heat of summer. Then I acknowledged my sin to You and did not cover up my iniquity. I said, "I will confess my transgressions to the LORD"—and You forgave the guilt of my sin** (based on Ps. 32:3–5).

Psalm 32 shows us that when we hold our sin inside and do not confess it to God, we suffer greatly. We feel emotionally bound up and stuck. We find freedom in confessing our sin. Is there a time when you confessed what you had done to someone else?

      ____ yes   ____ no

Did you find relief?

      ____ yes   ____ no

How? (such as going to my best friend to let him know about a rumor that I had passed on about someone else. He comforted me by letting me know that he didn't think it was nearly as big a deal as I had made it out to be. And he encouraged me to go back to the person and ask forgiveness for starting this rumor.)

_____

_____

_____

5. King Solomon's advice in this proverb is an important element of the fifth step. Sin cannot be covered over. There will always be consequences:

> **He who covers his sins will not prosper,**
> **But whoever confesses and forsakes them will have mercy** (Prov. 28:13).

____ I know that stuffing (hiding) my sins is not healthy.
____ I know that as I confess my sins I will find mercy.
____ Confession is the right thing to do. I will do it. I will confess specific sins.

6. James, the author of the Epistle of James, lays out some practical suggestions to the early Christian church. In his "sermon" he makes it clear that we need to **get into the habit of admitting your sins to each other and praying for each other** (based on James 5:16).

Choose the one that best describes how you feel:

____ I am afraid to do this. I don't know why but I am.

____ I would love to do this, but I don't know how.

____ This sounds like a good idea, but I am not ready yet.

7. Jesus gave a direct challenge to His audience about the use of their gifts. His words had a ring of urgency: **"People don't light a lamp and then hide it or put it under a bowl; instead, they put it on the lampstand so that others may see the light as they come in"** (based on Luke 11:33–34).

____ It's really hard for me to tell people about my good qualities or talents. I feel arrogant when I do that.

____ I want to share myself, my history, and my gifts with other people.

____ I am eager to put my "light" out for others to see.

Doing Step Five

After reading through these Scriptures you can probably see that God knew that each of us would sin (fall short of His desire for us) and therefore He wrote a process like Step Five into the Scriptures so we could be forgiven and released from the guilt and shame that result from sinful behavior.

Step Five is a natural part of the spiritual process. How do you feel about it now?

I'm most anxious about sharing myself honestly with

____ God.

____ another person.

____ myself.

In sharing myself with another person, I'm afraid of

____ being criticized.

____ being condemned.

____ being known for who I really am.

____ being rejected.

____ being judged.

When you have really tried to let someone else know the real you, what has been your experience?

_____

_____

_____

Making Step Five My Own

This section provides you with a format for integrating your feelings, responses to questions, and what you learned from this step, the Scriptures, and your group meetings.

Date, day, and time of your writings:

_____

1. At this point in my life, the major area that I am working on (for instance, being more conscious of my sins and confessing them as soon as they are brought to mind):

_____

_____

2. Major insights I was given into my life through this step (how important it is for me to share myself with another person): _____

_____

_____

_____

3. The scriptural passage that spoke to me most clearly in this step (It's not the healthy who need the doctor.):

_____

_____

The one word that has been most important to me in this chapter (Share—I will share with another person who I really am.):

_____

_____

4. The major discovery about Jesus Christ that I was given in this step (He has not come to condemn me but to forgive me.):

_____

_____

5. The strongest feeling I have as I have worked this step (Anxiety—because I know I am not good at sharing with others):

_____

6. The action I feel called to take as a result of working this step (Go to share with another—that's why I feel anxious.):

_____

7. The good news for me in this step and these passages (I know I can do this and I will.):

_____

CHAPTER 6

READY

▼

Step Six:

I am entirely ready to

have Jesus Christ

heal all those areas

of my life that need

His touch.

amie had been coming to meetings because she felt she was addicted to relationships. She said she had an empty spot in her life and she didn't feel good about herself.

For many years, Jamie knew that she didn't get along well with people. She had no close friends. Once in a while she developed a friendship with someone, but the friendship would be "sabotaged," as she put it, by her own "crazy" behavior. While she felt she was inviting the person to come closer, she was at the same time pushing her away.

Though she wanted intimacy, she did things to avoid it. Whenever anyone got close to her, she did something to make the relationship undesirable for the other person.

This fear of intimacy showed up in her marriage relationship as well. Though her marriage had no major problems, it had little joy. Her husband, Al, had resigned himself to having a fairly platonic relationship with Jamie. It was not what he wanted, but he felt helpless and hopeless about any more than that ever developing. He moved into a phase of "doing his own thing" while she did hers.

At age thirty-eight, Jamie saw her thirteen-year marriage falling apart. Al was becoming more demanding. She wanted to meet his needs but did not know how to do it. She had withdrawn into herself more than ever.

Hope came to Jamie when she began attending a group that was working on the material in this book. The critical circumstances in her life compelled her to find some answers.

Unfortunately we are always driven by pain. We hear better when we are suffering. Jamie had to face the facts. She was unhappy. She was contributing to her husband's unhappiness. (It took her a long time to understand that she was not responsible for his unhappiness, but contributing to it. He is responsible for his own happiness, she has learned the hard way).

She had no close friends. She had pushed them all away. "Why am I living

93

life like this? Why do I do this? What makes me want to be close to people and then push them away when they come close?'' she asked in one of the group meetings.

Jamie had taken an important step toward recovery. She was owning her personality type, and she was admitting to who she really is. She was ready, through the painful circumstances of her life, to make some needed changes.

''I wasn't ready six months ago. I have had several crises in my life, but none of them has been major enough to make me want to change. Now, I want to change. I know I have to change,'' she said. ''I am disgusted with my own life. Something has to give. I need to do something before I lose my husband and family.''

And the sixth step helped Jamie change. After she and her husband came to see me, I suggested that she read the first fifteen chapters of the Gospel of Luke. Luke was a physician, and so his gospel is filled with stories of how Jesus healed people who needed His touch.

One particular story made a great deal of sense to her. That story and the following exercises helped her identify herself, her needs, and the fact that Jesus could heal her.

What the Bible Says about Step Six

One Sabbath day Jesus was teaching in one of the synagogues, and a woman was there who had been ill for eighteen years. She had a spirit of weakness. She was bent over double and was unable to straighten up properly. She could not hold her head erect.

This woman stepped into Jesus' life out of nowhere. Little was known about her then. Little is known about her to this day. No one seemed to know for sure what her problem was. They felt sorry for her and felt helpless but simply accepted this posture as normal for her.

When Jesus noticed her, He called her and said, ''You are set free from your illness!'' And He put His hands upon her, and at once she stood upright and praised God.

Jesus must have known the private agony this woman had gone through because of her illness. He knew her need for healing. He touched her and set her free immediately (based on Luke 13:10–13).

1. Check the statements which are true about this woman:
___ She was eighteen years old.

____ She was bent over double.
____ She was unable to straighten up.
____ Jesus came to her home.
____ Jesus told her she would be set free from her illness.
____ She praised God.

2. Check the statements which are true about you:
____ I am bent over double.
____ I have a pain/problem that has been with me for a long time.
____ I am entirely ready to have Jesus touch me and make my life different.
____ I want to be entirely ready, but I don't know how.
____ Ready for what? I don't understand.

3. When Jesus says, "You are free from your illness," he means
____ "Find a way to straighten up, lady, and then I'll help you with your illness."
____ What He says.
____ The woman has to stay doubled over until she says she is sorry for everything she ever did wrong (repents).
____ He touched and healed her because He loved her, and He didn't expect anything in return from her.

Doing Step Six

Then I asked Jamie to think about the areas in which she needed Jesus' healing touch. I suggest that you think about that also.

1. Area(s) of your life in which you most need healing today:
____ Physical (For instance, I need help in getting more exercise, in watching what I eat more carefully, with my neckache.):

_____

_____

____ Mental (I do not feel very stable mentally right now. I feel bogged down and out of balance.)

_____

_____

___ Emotional (I feel drained or numb. I don't have anything to give to anyone else.):

_____

_____

___ Spiritual (I try hard to have more intimacy with God, but God seems so far away; or I don't devote any time at all to my relationship with God and I want this to change.):

_____

_____

___ Relational (For instance, I am having a terrible time communicating with my husband; or I have not spoken to my brother in five years.):

_____

_____

2. In order to have these areas of my life healed I need:
___ To have more pain—I don't hurt enough yet.
___ I need time and some solitude to sort things out.
___ I need to go back to steps four and five for a while longer
___ Nothing. I am ready and eager.

3. Believing in Jesus Christ and His power to touch and heal me is:
___ Very difficult for me. I don't feel worthy of His healing touch.
___ Frightening. That's getting too close for me.
___ Far fetched. Jesus doesn't do that kind of thing anymore.
___ Very easy. I've experienced His healing touch and power before.
___ I have little doubt about Jesus and His power to heal.

Finally, I suggested that Jamie read the following encouraging story from the Scriptures to see if she could find herself in it.

> **Jesus went back to Cana in Galilee where He had miraculously changed the water into wine. There was an important court official there whose son was sick at Capernaum. Hearing that Jesus had arrived in Galilee, the official went and pleaded with Him to come to Capernaum and cure his son, who was at the point of death.**
>
> **Jesus said, "Go home. Your son will live." The man believed what Jesus had said and started on his way; and while he was still on the journey back, his servants met him with the news that his boy was alive.**

He asked them when the boy had begun to recover. "The fever left him yesterday," they said, "at about one o'clock." The father realized that this was exactly the time when Jesus had said, "Your son will live."

He and all his household believed in Jesus (based on John 4:46–54).

1. From everything I can gather from this reading, the court official was:
____ Desperate to have his son healed.
____ Mildly concerned about his son's health.
____ Ready to do anything that Jesus would suggest.
____ Entirely ready for Jesus to intervene in the life of his son.

2. What is most impressive to me about this true story is:
____ The faith of the court official. When Jesus told him to go home, he believed and started on his way.
____ The fact that Jesus healed his son from a distance. He did not need to be present for the son to be healed.
____ The healing Jesus did.

3. The most important thing I've learned about Jesus through this reading is:
____ His word is good. When He said, "Go home. Your son will live," the court official could believe what He said and act on it.
____ Jesus' power to heal.
____ The authority that Jesus has. When He says something, it happens.
____ How timely His intervention was.
____ Jesus is capable of healing all those areas of our lives that need His touch. I believe He is waiting for me to come to Him, as the court official did.

4. The most important thing I've learned about myself through this reading is:
____ I need healing. I'm ready.
____ I believe Jesus can heal me.
____ If Jesus tells me to do something, I will do it without hesitation.
____ I need more time to think about all of this.

Making Step Six My Own

This section provides you with a format for integrating your feelings, your responses to questions, and what you learned from this step, the Scriptures, and your group meetings.

Date, day, and time of your writings:

_____

1. At this point in my life, the major area that I am working on (For instance, I am working on letting Jesus heal me emotionally.):

_____

_____

2. Major insights I was given into my life through this step (Until I looked at this step, I didn't realize how much I need God's healing.):

_____

_____

_____

_____

3. The scriptural passage that spoke to me most clearly in this step (the woman who needed Jesus' healing touch):

_____

   The one word that has been most important to me in this chapter (healing—I need and want healing):

_____

_____

4. The major discovery about Jesus Christ that I was given in this step (the reminder that He is the Great Healer):

_____

_____

5. The strongest feeling I have as I have worked this step (hope that I can someday become a whole person):

_____

6. The action I feel called to take as a result of working this step (pray more and receive God's blessings):

_____

7. The good news for me in this step and these passages (the hope I find in prayer):

_____

CHAPTER 7

ASKING FOR
HEALING

▼

Step Seven:

I humbly ask Jesus

Christ to change my

weaknesses into

strengths so that I will

become more like Him.

I've spent several years working through Step Seven. I am in need of Jesus' healing touch in several major areas of my life. I have asked for His help and intervention. I am grateful for the healing He has already done. I am hopeful about the gradual and gentle changes He is making in me and will make in me.

I have shared with you my addiction to ideal-aholism. This is a serious and often devastating mind-set and compulsion. As an ideal-aholic I think that the world and everything in the world should be ideal—perfect. Because I have such high ideals, I was often disappointed, frustrated, even angry. Injustice, war, the need for prisons, divorce, poverty, crime—these are just a few examples of the types of situations I was convinced *should* not be here.

Should is an important word. It is a word I grew up with. Whether it was said often or not, I cannot remember. I do know that somehow I got the clear message: I should do this and that; and things should not be this way or that.

This is a subtle form of denial. If things are not as they should be and I am unwilling to let them be as they are, I am living in denial. It is true that it would be great if there were no crime, no criminals, and no prisons. But that is not reality.

In the past I was easily shocked by news of some of the behavior of our great heroes. Now, nothing could shake me.

Years ago I might have had a heart attack if I had heard the news I have recently heard about Christian leaders. I was not very realistic about human life. I was naive. I didn't allow much room for the human dimension. I blindly trusted people who had not earned my trust. (In simple language, this is called stupidity.)

It has been helpful for me to use this label "ideal-aholic" because it lets me be honest about areas of my life that have made me uncomfortable. I see this label as diagnostic, and 90 percent of the solution to any problem is good diagnosis. This is what I take to the Lord and ask for His healing touch about. This

103

ideal-aholism has three parts to it. The Lord is working in all three parts, changing them from weaknesses into strengths.

1. He is changing my weakness of judgmentalism into a strength of intuition. Instead of walking into a room, looking at some of the people, and making judgments about them, I am learning from God how to look at them with compassion, pray for them, and reach out to them. He is teaching me to accept them as they are. He is alerting me to use this great gift of intuition that He has given me.

The intuition is like radar and X-ray vision. Within a short time, I can "sense" where certain people are and what kinds of words of encouragement I might be able to give to them.

My intuition always gives me clear messages about specific situations where I need guidance. Some years ago when I was offered a position of leadership, my intuition told me this would not be good. I promptly informed the person this would not be a good position for me. I responded to my intuition and the results were good.

God is helping me to use more intuition and do less judging. This intuition is a great gift that I ignored for years. Now I use it all the time. In counseling situations, I can get to the heart of matters in no time. I can see through the peripherals and quickly move right into the real problem, not just the symptoms.

On the other hand, my judgmentalism would put a label on a person because of external things and never develop enough of a relationship for the heart matters to emerge.

God is touching me. He is healing me. He is moving me toward a freer, more accepting, and more Spirit-led lifestyle. He is transforming my judgmentalism into healthy intuition.

2. The second part of my ideal-aholism is perfectionism. In my early years I often heard the message, "You can do better than that." The message was true, but the long-range impact has been severe.

I don't remember hearing, "That was really well done" or "You did good on that" or "It's wonderful that you got four A's." Instead I heard, "You can do better."

For more than twenty years I have been moving away from perfectionism. I am moving towards a more spontaneous, "leave things as they are," leisurely lifestyle. This was hard work for me as I became aware of how my perfectionism was killing me. Although the message of perfectionism is a good message, it can be destructive when taken to its extreme.

When I was younger, I felt I couldn't come to God until I had a better, cleaner life. I avoided some people because I hadn't done enough work on improving myself to be ready to present myself to them. I had given myself a message: You're not good enough as you are; you're inadequate; work on yourself; shape up some more so you can be acceptable to God and others.

Perfectionism is bondage to self-imposed standards, family messages, and cultural values. God is delivering me from this bondage into His great freedom. One of the ways He does it is through Scripture.

Paul asked a hard question in his letter to the Colossians. **"If you have really died with Christ to the principles of this world, why do you still let its rules dictate to you, as though you were still living in the world?"** (based on 2:20).

In his letter to the Galatians he says, **"When Christ freed us, He meant us to stay free. Stand firm then and do not submit again to the yoke of slavery"** (based on 5:1). And in his letter to the Romans he wrote, **"Don't let the world squeeze you into its mold, but let God remold your minds from within"** (based on 12:2).

How can we do this? How can we be set free from the squeeze of perfection-ism and other cultural pressures? Step Seven gives us the answer—humbly ask Jesus Christ to change our weaknesses into strengths. We can ask with confi-dence, not because we want something just for ourselves, but because our sincere desire is to become more like Him.

Paul says in Colossians 3:1–3 to look for the things that are in heaven, where Christ is, sitting at God's right hand. This is where our eyes should be focused—not on ourselves, not on our problems, not on our way of doing things.

3. The third area of ideal-aholism is work-aholism. If I am to be an ideal person and provider, it means I must work all the time. According to this way of thinking, work is primary. Relationships are secondary.

Work/profession comes first, this system says; self, second; spouse, third; children, fourth; and God, fifth. This is often the order of priorities in this world's system.

Work-aholism is a symptom of a performance-based mentality. My value comes through what I do, accomplish, own, or control, this mentality says. My identity is based on these externals, not on who I am.

From God's perspective, the opposite is true. God looks at the heart. He looks at character. He wants us to become more like Jesus Christ. Jesus Christ is not a driven, performance-based person. From everything I can gather in my reading of the New Testament, He was never in a hurry. He had no great plans. His life was simple. He had one purpose in life—to die on the cross for our sins so that He can save us.

Performance-based identity or grace-based identity—we can choose. The world has us convinced that performance is all that matters, that grace is meaningless. I need to be healed from this way of thinking. I humbly ask Jesus to change this part of me.

Ultimately all that counts is whether we have loved—as Jesus loves. Have I allowed Him to love me? Have I allowed Him to use me as a vessel to love and serve others? Have I loved Him, myself, my spouse, my family, my neighbor? Nothing else matters in comparison. Only love counts.

What about You?

Jesus can change all dimensions of our lives. We, however, have a part to play in the process. Our part is to be honest and identify our weaknesses, then humbly ask for His help. The rest is up to Him. He will respond in His own way and time. He encourages us to ask and seek. His promise is that "if anyone thirsts, let that person come to Me and drink." Jesus will help us.

What are your greatest areas of weakness right now? Check the statements that apply to you.

____ I tend to criticize others.
____ I sometimes lie to defend myself.
____ I tend to dislike people who have different beliefs than I do or come from different backgrounds.
____ I tend to judge people quickly.
____ I sometimes want to do things I know are wrong.
____ Sometimes I am attracted to a person other than my spouse.
____ I tend to envy my neighbors or others at work when something good happens to them.

____ _____

____ _____

____ _____

Are you willing to humbly ask Jesus Christ to change those weaknesses into strengths? Do you sincerely desire to become more like Christ?

A primary goal for every Christian is to become more like Christ, to be more filled with Him and the Holy Spirit so that we can lovingly serve Him and others. To become more like Christ, we need to identify and deal with our weaknesses.

Every person has strengths. Every person has weaknesses. Jesus Christ can change our weaknesses into strengths.

Step Six reminds us of how disgusting our behavior can sometimes be. Step

Seven helps us realize the hope that we have in Jesus Christ—that He can take these weak areas of our lives and make them into strengths.

What is it that you want Jesus to heal for you right now (for instance, my relationship with a friend, my headaches, my lack of trust, a bad experience in my past)?

_____

As I read the letters from the apostle Paul, I am amazed at how much he went through. He was one of the greatest leaders history has ever known. Like all great leaders, he had opponents, great struggles, and personal issues to deal with. In the passage below, he describes one of these as the "thorn in his side." He says this thorn was given to him so that he might not become proud.

No one is really sure what that thorn was, but his own testimony says that this weakness ended up being a strength for Paul:

> **To keep me from becoming conceited because of these surpassingly great revelations, there was given me a thorn in my flesh, a messenger of Satan, to torment me. Three times I pleaded with the Lord to take it away from me. But He said to me, "My grace is sufficient for you, for my power is made perfect in weakness." Therefore I will boast all the more gladly about my weaknesses so that Christ's power may rest on me. That is why, for Christ's sake, I delight in weaknesses, in insults, in hardships, in persecutions, in difficulties. For when I am weak, then I am strong** (based on 2 Cor. 12.7–10).

After reading this passage I:

____ Understand better why some people might be given "thorns."

____ Understand better why God might not answer some of my prayers (that it's best for me to have "thorns" in my life to keep me humble).

____ Believe God's grace is sufficient and His power is made perfect in weakness.

____ Believe that when I am weakest, that's really when I am strong. Jesus wants me to humbly trust Him and call on Him.

Jesus can transform our weaknesses into strengths, just as He did Paul's.

Identify one area of weakness in your life that Jesus has already transformed into a strength:

____ I am becoming less judgmental and more accepting.

____ My loneliness motivates me to take initiative in being with others.

____ When I feel guilty, I feel motivated to confess my sin.

____ Because of some bad past experiences with adults, I can now understand and help others who suffer from similar abuse.

____ Jesus has changed my fear of being alone into great times of solitude and prayer.

____ I used to _____, but now I _____.

____ _____

____ _____

____ _____

____ _____

Jesus Changes the Life of One Man

Jesus went up to a Jewish festival in Jerusalem. At the Sheep Pool in Jerusalem there is a building with five covered porches surrounding it. Under these porches were crowds of sick, lame, blind, and paralyzed people. They were all there waiting for the water to move, for at intervals the angel of the Lord came down into the pool and the water was disturbed. The first person to enter the water after this disturbance was cured of any ailment that person suffered.

One man there had an illness which had lasted thirty-eight years, and when Jesus saw him lying there and knew he had been in this condition for a long time, He said, "Do you want to be healed?"

"I can't," the sick man said, "for I have no one to help me into the pool at the movement of the water. While I'm trying to get there, someone else always gets in ahead of me."

Jesus told him, "Stand up, roll up your sleeping mat and go home!" Instantly the man was healed. He rolled up his mat and began walking (based on John 5:1–9).

Think about this miraculous healing with me.

1. Which best describes the man at the pool?
____ He was persistent; he must have sincerely sought healing.
____ He was psychologically sick, not physically sick.
____ He was extremely ill; that's why Jesus singled him out.
____ He deserved Jesus' help after waiting for thirty-eight years.
____ It's hard to know much about this person from this reading.

2. In what ways are you like the man at the pool?
____ I have paralysis of the brain much of the day.

_____ I am sick.

_____ I am psychologically sick.

_____ I am holding on to things inside that make me feel sick sometimes.

_____ I want to be healed.

_____ I have gone to the "place of healing" many times and nothing has happened to me.

3. When Jesus asked the man at the pool if he wanted to become whole, He was asking him:

_____ If he wanted to become healthy physically.

_____ If he wanted to become healthy psychologically.

_____ If he wanted to become spiritually healthy.

_____ If he wanted his whole life to be integrated, sound, and healthy.

_____ If he wanted things to stay the way they were.

4. When Jesus asks you if you want to become whole, how do you answer?

_____ Not yet—I'm not ready.

_____ I don't know.

_____ I'm ready to become whole. What is my part in the process?

_____ I really like my life the way it is, even though parts of it are unhealthy.

_____ Please come, Lord Jesus, and make me whole.

5. What strikes me most about this passage is:

_____ The fact that Jesus came to touch one person in that crowd.

_____ Jesus' offer to make the man whole.

_____ The power that Jesus has to make whole.

_____ The offer that I feel Jesus is making to me.

_____ The fact that Jesus would even bother spending time with an insignificant person like this man.

6. Which of the following propositions seems most to agree with your perspective today?

_____ The more I let go, the more wholesome I become.

_____ The more I hang on to control, the more my health dissipates.

_____ Wholeness (wellness) comes through relationships with God, self, and others.

_____ Ultimately, only Jesus can make us well and whole.

_____ Jesus is waiting for my response to His question "Do you want to become whole?"

Jesus has the power to make each of us whole. He said so Himself. Let's listen to Him as He speaks to us through the record of His words in the Bible.

What the Bible Says about Step Seven

Jesus promises to bring living water to those who believe in Him. He has just finished telling the crowds gathered at the Festival of Lights that He would only physically be with them a short time, that they would look for Him and not find Him.

Yet Jesus Christ is with us today. He will respond to our humble plea. He will provide us with living, healing water.

> **On the last and most important day of the Festival, Jesus stood in the crowd and cried out, "If anyone is thirsty, let that person come to Me! Let the person come to Me and drink, whoever believes in Me. Fountains of living water will flow from within that person's breast." He was speaking of the Spirit which those who believe in Him were to receive; for there was no spirit as yet because Jesus had not yet been glorified** (based on John 7:37–39).

1. Write below a few words that describe your thoughts or feelings after reading this passage of Scripture:

_____

_____

_____

2. Jesus' words, "If anyone is thirsty, let that person come to Me," evoke the following reaction from me:
____ I am grateful that I have accepted His invitation. I have come to Him.
____ I'm not sure what this means.
____ I don't know how to come to Christ.
____ I must not be thirsty.
____ I want to come to Jesus Christ. I want Him to change my weaknesses into strengths, but I don't know how to do it.

3. When I hear/read Jesus' words, "from that person's breast will flow fountains of living water,"
____ I don't understand.
____ I think Jesus means that out of Him fountains of living water will flow into His followers.
____ This must mean that fountains of living water will flow within the one who believes and trusts in Christ.

___ I'm not sure of the meaning of this passage. I do know that something good is happening to me as I meditate on it.

The Power Jesus Gives to Each of Us

In the passage below, Jesus is preparing His disciples for His departure that will come very soon. He is teaching them about what life will be like without His human presence. He gives them an array of promises, promises that are true for us, His disciples today. If we will but ask in Jesus' name, Jesus will respond to our prayer. He says:

> **I tell you, truly, whoever believes in Me will do the same works as I do Myself; in fact, that follower of Mine will do even greater works because I am going to the Father.**
>
> **Whatever you ask for in My name, I will do so that the Father may be glorified in the Son. If you ask for anything in My name, I will do it.**
>
> **If you love Me you will keep My commandments.**
>
> **I will ask the Father, and He will give you another Advocate to be with you forever, that Spirit of Truth whom the world cannot receive since it neither sees Him nor knows Him; but you know Him** (based on John 14:12–17).

1. Write below a few words that describe your thoughts or feelings after reading this passage of Scripture:

_____

_____

_____

2. Jesus said, **"Whoever believes in Me will perform the same works as I do Myself, he will do even greater works"** (based on John 14:12).
___ I'm not sure Jesus said this. It's hard to believe.
___ This is impossible.
___ This is possible if God is working through me.
___ I am encouraged by this promise.
___ I am confident that God can use me as I am—with my weaknesses and my strengths.
___ I am eager to do the same or greater works than Jesus did.

3. Jesus said, **"Whatever you ask in My name, that I will do"** (John 14:13).
___ This is not something Jesus said. This couldn't be.

___ I believe Jesus said it. But I never ask for anything in his name.
___ I do this all the time. Asking in Jesus' name comes naturally for me.
___ I want to learn more about this.
___ I need more experience in this.

4. Jesus said, **"I will pray the Father, and He will give you another Helper, that He may abide with you forever . . . He dwells with you and will be in you"** (John 14:16–17).
___ I am grateful for this. I know Jesus is with me.
___ At times I have known this is true, but those times are rare.
___ I want to experience more of this for myself.
___ The Holy Spirit has strengthened me and encouraged me with His presence.

As Jesus promised in John 14:16–17, the power of the Holy Spirit is available to anyone who has accepted Christ as Savior. So that we can understand this power available to us, let's look at what the Bible says about the Holy Spirit.

The Comforter, The Holy Spirit

The Scriptures listed below are important, in-depth references to the Person and work of the Holy Spirit. These passages will help you discover the transforming power that the Holy Spirit gives as we humbly ask Jesus Christ to change our weaknesses into strengths. Please meditate on these and write about how they apply to your life.

Jesus has just taught His disciples how to pray. Ask, knock, and seek, He has told them. In that context He says, **"If you then, being evil, know how to give good gifts to your children, how much more will your heavenly Father give the Holy Spirit to those who ask Him"** (Luke 11:13).

___ This has happened to me. I have asked for the Holy Spirit. He has come, and He has filled me with Himself.
___ I didn't know I had to ask. I just thought the Holy Spirit automatically came to live in my heart and empower me for life.
___ I don't know what to make of this passage.
___ I want the Holy Spirit. I am asking the Father to give Him to me.

___ _____

2. Jesus was about to leave the earth. In the following passage He is giving His very last words to His disciples: **"He told them not to leave Jerusalem but to wait for what the Father had promised. 'You have heard Me speak about this before. John baptized with water, but you, not many days from now, will be**

baptized with the Holy Spirit. You will receive power when the Holy Spirit comes on you''' (based on Acts 1:1–8).

___ I'm waiting. I'm not going anywhere. For too long, I have been running around without the Power described in this passage.

___ I have been given this Power. I have received the Holy Spirit. He is changing my weaknesses into strengths and using me.

___ I've waited for a long time and nothing has happened.

___ God, please come and fill me with Your Holy Spirit.

_____

Jesus taught His disciples about the importance and role of the Holy Spirit. This is important teaching for me. As I humbly seek the Lord He will enable me to become more like Him. He said, **"The Helper, the Holy Spirit, whom the Father will send in My name, He will teach you all things, and bring to your remembrance all things that I said to you"** (John 14:26).

___ Jesus has sent the Holy Spirit to me.

___ The Holy Spirit is teaching me everything.

___ The Holy Spirit is reminding me of all that Jesus said and did and is doing.

In his letter to young Timothy, one of his closest friends and companions, Paul describes the gift of the Holy Spirit. He says, **God's gift of the Holy Spirit is not a spirit of timidity, but the Spirit of power, love, and self-control** (based on 2 Tim. 1:7).

___ Help me to be bold, not timid, Lord Jesus.

___ I believe Your power can change all of my weaknesses into strengths.

___ Your Spirit will fill me with love and power and self-control. Thank you, Lord Jesus.

_____

Doing Step Seven

Now that you know the power that Jesus has to change your weaknesses into strengths, think again about Step Seven: I humbly ask Jesus Christ to change my weaknesses into strengths so that I will become more like Him.

—Step Seven says, "I humbly ask Jesus Christ . . ."

___ It is hard for me to ask anyone for anything. I can do all things on my own.

___ Asking doesn't pay. I've tried. It just hasn't worked for me.

___ Jesus doesn't have time for me and my petty problems. Why bother asking Him for help?

___ I have asked. He is responding.

_____ I have asked. He has responded!

—Step Seven says, ''I humbly ask Jesus Christ to change my weaknesses into strengths.''

_____ I believe He can do this, but I'm not sure I want it done.

_____ I still don't know my weaknesses and strengths.

_____ I have experienced this. Jesus has and is changing my weaknesses into strengths. Praise Him!

—Step Seven says, ''I humbly ask Jesus Christ to change my weaknesses into strengths so that I will become more like Him.''

_____ I want to become more like Jesus.

_____ I want to become more like Jesus but am doubtful it could ever happen.

_____ I would give anything (everything) to become more like Christ.

_____ I know that I have become more like Him in at least a few small ways.

Read through the prayer below as you ask Jesus to turn your strengths into weaknesses.

The Step Seven Prayer

Lord Jesus,

Through these Steps, I come to You with a better understanding of my strengths, weaknesses, and shortcomings. I come to You now with a better awareness of who I am. I am more aware of my strengths and weaknesses. I am more in touch with my gifts.

Now, more than ever, I am alert to the shortcomings and sin in my life. I know I have sinned, Lord. Please forgive me. Please do more than forgive me. Please change me so that I can become more like You.

I have come now to another point in my life where I really need You. Please change me. Please change my weaknesses into strengths.

When I want to criticize, please help me to see good things in others.

When I want to lie, please help me to be honest.

When I hate, please help me to love.

When I want to judge others, please have mercy on me, and give me that same mercy for others.

When I want to do wrong, help me to do right.

When I lust, please deliver me.

When I am envious, help me to be grateful for what I have.

Lord, please change me. Please take away my bad habits, my compulsions, my addictions. Replace them all with those good things that come from You.

Mostly, Lord, please change my heart. Please change my mind. Please change my attitude.

I promise to do my part, to change what I can. But I know that only You have the power to change me and make me more like Yourself.

I pray that You would do all these things, Lord Jesus, in Your name.

Making Step Seven My Own

This section provides you with a format for integrating your feelings, responses to questions, and what you learned from this step, from the Scriptures, and in your group meetings.

Date, day, and time of your writings:

_____

1. At this point in my life, the major area that I am working on (For instance, I am humbly asking Jesus and others for what I need.):

_____

_____

2. Major insights I was given into my life through this step (I am ready to have Jesus heal me.):

_____

_____

_____

_____

3. The scriptural passage that spoke to me most clearly in this step ("These and greater things You will do."):

_____

The one word that has been most important to me in this chapter (Humbly—I humbly ask Jesus Christ to heal me.):

_____

_____

4. The major discovery about Jesus Christ that I was given in this step (Jesus heals people one by one; He will come to heal me.):

_____

_____

5. The strongest feeling I have as I work this step (Humility—I realize that I need to be more real and more human.):

_____

6. The action I feel called to take as a result of working this step (Ask for help.):

_____

7. The good news for me in this step and these passages (My weaknesses will be changed into strengths.):

_____

CHAPTER 8

SHARING
THE HEALING

▼

Step Eight:

I make a list of the people I have hurt and become willing to go to them to mend the relationship.

hen everything else is gone, relationships will stand. Nothing is as important as our family and friends. Most families have a history of broken relationships and have forgotten how broken they are. When one person in the family begins to deal with these issues, relationships within the family can improve, but not without cost or pain.

The relationships we have we need to keep. The ones we have lost, we need to work to restore. The ones that we don't yet have, we need to establish.

The first chapter of this book mentions Rita, who had an alcoholic father. She was in her late thirties, was married, and had two children.

Because her romantic and sexual life with her husband was quite ''chilly'' for many years, they both grew into a system of detachment and tolerance. They didn't really fight. But they weren't close. They lived together as ''roommates.'' He had his own lifestyle. She had hers. They ate meals and occasionally did other things together. They slept in the same bed, but on opposite sides, both with their own reading material.

Neither one of them liked this lifestyle. John, the husband, had pulled away more and more. He had repeatedly expressed his frustration and hopelessness. He had all but given up. They had been to counseling, but there had been no major breakthrough until recently.

Recognizing that both of them contributed to their ''cooled'' relations, John and Rita both acknowledged that one partner's background can have a greater impact on shaping the marriage. Most often, unfortunately, that's the negative background.

As Rita said, she came from an alcoholic family. For years, she had stuffed her feelings about it. Her memory of it had been darkened. She chose, like many adult children of alcoholics, to ignore what she went through. As she forgot, she hoped that the past would not affect the way she was now, especially in her relationship with John.

She was in love with John. She felt so bad about the way things were between them. She had no intention of hurting him or being distant from him. In fact, this was the farthest thing from her mind. She wanted and needed to be close to him, and she agonized over the pain she was causing him.

At her weekly support group, Rita listened to others tell part of their stories, and she shared some of hers. Some weeks she said nothing, but gradually, week by week, she grew stronger and healthier. The group listened, stood by her, and prayed for her. All participants were in this process together. Neither a clique nor a gossip group, they were there to support and encourage one another.

Rita gradually began to peel away the layers of darkness. She did this gently and at a pace that was right for her. Patiently she let the light shine into her dark spots, one spot at a time. The group never pushed her to do anything. They were there for her in the group setting and available to her outside group meetings. John stood faithfully by as Rita worked all this through.

As her life story unfolded, Rita saw many ways that her past affected her relationship with John. She was afraid of men. She had no reason to be afraid of John, but she could not control her fear. This fear kept her from being close to John and others. She was guarded and suspicious about men, and she kept her distance from John. Gentle and careful as he was, she still hesitated to give herself to him physically or emotionally. She wanted what John offered, but she was afraid to take it.

While she was afraid of men, she was also attracted to them. She sometimes had overwhelming feelings for other men. She had longings for intimacy, but didn't know how to address those longings in her marriage. She was often tempted to have an affair. She sometimes flirted with men just to "test the waters" and see whether she might still be attractive to them.

She learned from experience that she could very easily find a partner for an affair. She "fell into" an "emotional affair" with one of the family's closest friends. "An emotional affair," she said, "is a relationship that has a strong psychological and spiritual bond, but no physical contact. Without knowing it, I developed a strong dependency on this other man, much more than my dependency on John. I knew it was an adulterous relationship in that I had nothing left to give John. I shared all my feelings, experiences, and thoughts with this other person."

This emotional affair didn't make sense to her. How could she intentionally keep her distance from John physically and emotionally and yet build a relationship with another man?

She loved John. She had hurt him a great deal in several ways. By fantasizing about other men, she could fulfill her desires and not need John for that part of her life.

John knew about the relationship Rita was having, but didn't think it was serious because he thought they didn't spend much time together. The relationship was much more serious for Rita because this emotional affair was weakening her marriage to John. Instead of sharing intimate thoughts with John, she shared them with her friend.

Rita liked this affair because she could completely control the relationship. She felt safe. She could call when she wanted. She could and did take the initiative. She could hang up the phone when she didn't want to talk or when she became uncomfortable. She was using the man. The affair was all on her terms. It was self-centered and was harmful to everyone involved.

Rita knew that she wanted a pure and faithful relationship with John and John alone. She also knew that her emotional affair was wrong, but she didn't want to break it. In fact, she found subtle delight in hurting John by having this "safe" affair. Ultimately, she discovered that she was punishing John for what had happened to her early in life. When she finally dealt with those things, she found the freedom to be intimate with John, an intimacy they both longed for. And she no longer needed—or even wanted—an emotional bond with another man.

Rita soon learned that John was at the top of her list of people whom she had harmed. And she learned that she had been harmed as well. Scripture tells us that we must forgive as well as seek forgiveness.

What the Bible Says about Forgiveness

Please read the following passages and select a response that most describes where you are right now.

Jesus gave His disciples teaching that they had never heard before. He spoke with authority. They listened. Perhaps His most difficult teaching was the one that follows. It is an important one as we think about those who have hurt us.

1. Jesus says, **"Love your enemies, do good to those who hate you, bless those who curse you, and pray for those who spitefully use you"** (Luke 6:27–28).
____ Without Your help, Lord Jesus, I cannot go back to those who have hurt me.
____ I need to make amends.
____ This is impossible for me. I want to do it, but cannot pray for or go to those who mistreated me.
____ I can't do this yet, but what I can do is clearly identify those who have hurt me.

2. In response to their expressed desire to pray, Jesus taught the disciples a pattern for prayer. Here is a portion of what is now entitled the "Lord's Prayer":

"Forgive us our debts,
As we forgive our debtors.
And do not lead us into temptation,
But deliver us from the evil one."
After He finished the prayer, Jesus added, "For if you forgive
men their trespasses, your heavenly Father will also forgive you.
But if you do not forgive men their trespasses, neither will your
Father forgive your trespasses" (Matt. 6:12–13a, 14–15).

____ I need God's forgiveness.
____ I need God's help in forgiving others.
____ I think I live dangerously if I do not forgive others.

3. Solomon, a wise Old Testament king, wrote most of the book of Proverbs.
One of his important proverbs says, **"Do not say, 'I'll pay you back for this
wrong!' Wait for the Lord, and He will deliver you. Do not say, 'I'll do to
him as he has done to me; I'll pay that person back for what he did'"** (based
on Prov. 20:22; 24:29).
____ This passage helps me with my feelings of resentment and revenge. It puts
them in perspective.
____ I am learning to let the Lord "deliver me."
____ I will let the Lord pay back a person who has wronged me. He will do what
is right.

4. Part of loving each other is being sure that the relationship is reconciled and
"together." People seek this unity, which is evidence that we are His disciples.
Jesus says, **"A new commandment I give to you, that you love one another; as
I have loved you, that you also love one another. By this all will know that
you are My disciples, if you have love for one another"** (John 13:34–35).
____ To love my brothers or sisters means I am reconciled with them.
____ If I love them, I will do what I can to make amends.
____ By the love we have for one another, the world will know we are Christ's
disciples.
Strange as it may seem, most people begin the work of Step Eight by making
amends with themselves. They gently recognize areas of their lives where they
have hurt themselves. For some this means they have been too hard on themselves, expecting too much and depriving themselves of a great deal. For others,
it has meant recognizing that they have not lived with integrity.
One man shared in a group recently that he has never really done anything
for himself. "I felt selfish whenever I bought something for myself. I unnecessar-

ily deprived myself of basic things that I need. I have made amends with myself about this. And now, once in a while, I buy myself a treat. I always buy myself a birthday present.''

Most people have at least one unreconciled relationship in their lives. As a person who is in a relationship with Jesus Christ, I know that I am loved and forgiven. I have the freedom to love and forgive others. I can take the initiative to mend the relationship, even if I am convinced I have not been the one responsible for breaking the relationship.

Reconciliation is the highest priority. In most cases it doesn't even matter who was right or who was wrong. As a Christian, I am responsible to make the move to reconcile.

> Lord Jesus, help me to do this step. I resent this person for what he has done to me. I know that You want our relationship to be restored. Years have gone by, and we still do not greet one another. This is not what You want from me or us. Please give me the courage to go to him. Help me to tell him I'm sorry. Give me the strength to ask his forgiveness. And then give me the faith to entrust all the results to You.

Doing Step Eight

I will make a list of the people I have hurt and become willing to go to them to mend the relationship.

Before trying to mend relationships, we need to list and reflect on those with whom we have broken or disturbed relationships. This is the most difficult challenge of Step Eight. I resist doing this, but I know I need to do it—for my own health and growth.

Sometimes I have been the one who caused the separation. I have hurt people, offended them, judged them, been critical of them, and distanced myself from them. Even when I have been hurt or wronged, I am aware that I was probably not entirely faultless. The only hope for restoring a wounded relationship is for one person to take the initiative to restore it. Unless it will be harmful to the other person, I know in my heart I must do everything I can to mend any broken relationship. However, mending a relationship can only be as successful as the two people working together make it. It takes the effort of both.

Make your list of people you have harmed. Begin with those you have hurt today. Gradually work your way back in time so that you include those you have hurt this past week, this month, this year. Please don't be embarrassed. We have all hurt someone. All of us need this step.

The List of Those I Have Hurt

My list of those I have hurt and with whom I want to mend a relationship.

Myself:

_____

_____

_____

Family:

_____

_____

_____

Friends:

_____

_____

_____

Relatives:

_____

_____

_____

Teachers:

_____

_____

_____

Pastors:

_____

_____

_____

Others:

_____

_____

_____

One man in the Bible gave his life to Jesus (did Step Three) and then felt compelled to make amends to those he had harmed. His name was Zacchaeus. As a tax collector in Jericho he had collected extra taxes so he could make more money.

The Tax Collector Who Took Step Eight

Jesus was making His way through Jericho when He found a wealthy man called Zacchaeus, a chief tax collector, who wanted to see what sort of person Jesus was. The crowd prevented him from doing so because he was very short. So he ran ahead and climbed up into a sycamore tree to get a view of Jesus as He was heading that way.

When Jesus reached the spot, He looked up and saw the man and said, "Zacchaeus, hurry and come down. I must be your guest today." So Zacchaeus hurriedly climbed down and gladly welcomed Him. But those standing by muttered their disapproval: "Now Jesus has gone to stay with a real sinner."

But Zacchaeus himself stopped and said to the Lord, "Look, sir, I will give half my property to the poor. And if I have cheated anybody out of anything, I will pay him back four times as much."

Jesus said to him, "Salvation has come to this house today. It is the lost that I came to seek and to save" (based on Luke 19:1–10).

1. Why do you think Zacchaeus was so anxious to see Jesus?
_____ He had everything else in life, and he needed some excitement.
_____ He did a fourth step with the Jericho Twelve-Step group and decided it was time to have his life changed.
_____ His life was empty.
_____ He was fed up with his own lifestyle. He knew it was wrong to cheat others. He knew he needed Jesus' help to change his behavior.

2. Jesus came for the
_____ rich and famous.
_____ short and funny.
_____ lost.
_____ religious people.

3. Zacchaeus's first vocal response to Jesus was:

___ I will give half my property to the poor.

___ If I've cheated anybody out of anything, I'll pay him back ten times.

___ I never hurt anybody.

___ I didn't do anything wrong.

4. Pretend you are Zacchaeus. You have met Jesus, and He has invited Himself to your house for lunch.

What was your reaction as He invited Himself? How does His visit make you feel? Does His presence remind you of the need to make amends (as it reminded Zach)? Do you sense Jesus' love for you? Do you feel ready to make amends because God has come to visit you and let you know that He accepts you as you are?

Open yourself up to be reminded of someone that you may have hurt quite a while ago. This is an act of maturity and a necessary part of growth. Maybe it was a lie that you told or a rumor that you started. Perhaps you slighted someone or insulted a family member or fellow worker. Look again at your list of behaviors in Step Four. Have you done something wrong to another person? The purpose of Step Eight is to get ready to mend the relationship with that person so that you can be free.

We do this process because it is the right thing to do right now, at this moment. It will take some courage, but getting it done will be worth it. You will be set free. We all need to be set free, to make amends, to make every effort to clean the slate. We all need the peace and relief that comes with knowing we have done our best to restore our damaged relationships.

To the Lord, relationships were primary. Jesus came to die for us so that our relationship with the Father could be restored. He came to break down the walls between us, God, and others.

We are all familiar with the scriptural text, **"If you bring your gift to the altar, and there remember that your brother [sister] has something against you, leave your gift there before the altar, and go...be reconciled to your brother [sister], and then come and offer your gift"** (Matt. 5:23–24). Step Eight is another way of reminding us that we need to be reconciled with our "brothers and sisters."

Making the list and being willing to mend these relationships is all we need to do in Step Eight. Step Nine is the action step where we actually go to that person.

But the second part of Step Eight is making a list of people who have hurt us. That was the second area Rita needed to consider.

Early in her life, Rita's father had verbally abused her. He had often called her names and belittled her. She remembered how shocked she felt as her father repeatedly told her, "You will never amount to anything. You are a no good, worthless, fat little wench."

These devastating words penetrated deeply into Rita's mind and heart. They were the words that she most often thought of as she was growing up, especially when things weren't going well for her. These words had great influence in shaping her self-esteem. Though she was never overweight, she always felt "fat" because of the powerful impact of her father's words.

Now, in her late thirties, Rita was confronting these words. She was letting her memory come back to life. She was listening again to her father's voice and his repetition of those words. She felt again the devastation that she felt as a thirteen-year-old girl. It hurt so bad. The name-calling cut right to her heart—even though she knew it wasn't true.

She wanted so much to trust her father then and now. She still wanted to love him and be loved by him. She looked up to him. She needed him. But almost every time she turned to him, he hurt and abused her.

Not only did he abuse her verbally, but, on three occasions that she could remember, he whipped her with a strap—once so badly that she could not go to school for two days. Instead of being her advocate, defender, and protector, her father was hostile.

As Rita unraveled all of this pain, she identified the specific people who had hurt her. She remembered the most important incidents surrounding that hurt. And she became willing to go to those people to let them know that she is aware of the consequences of what has happened and she is willing to forgive them, hard as that will be for her.

Think about your own life and make a second list—the people who have hurt you.

The List of Those Who Have Hurt Me

My list of those who have hurt me:

_____

_____

_____

Family:

_____

_____

_____

Friends:

_____

_____

_____

Relatives:

_____

_____

_____

Teachers:

_____

_____

_____

Pastors:

_____

_____

_____

Others:

_____

_____

_____

Forgiveness is not easy. Without Jesus' help, it seems impossible. But with God's help, all things are possible. Let's look at what He said about forgiveness.

Making Step Eight My Own

This section provides you with a format for integrating your feelings, your responses to questions, and what you learned from this step, from the Scriptures, and in your group meetings.

Date, day, and time of your writings:

_____

1. At this point in my life, the major area that I am working on (For instance, I am making amends with a former employer.):

_____
_____

2. Major insights I was given into my life through this step (As I forgive, I will be forgiven.):

_____
_____
_____
_____

3. The scriptural passage that spoke to me most clearly in this step (Love one another as I have loved you.):

_____
_____

The one word that has been most important to me in this chapter (Initiative—I am responsible to take initiative in reconciling the relationship.):

_____
_____

4. The major discovery about Jesus Christ that I was given in this step (Jesus wants me to love my enemies; He demonstrated how to do it.):

_____
_____

5. The strongest feeling I have as I work this step (Fear—I am afraid to try to be reconciled.):

_____

6. The action I feel called to take as a result of working this step (I feel I must take the initiative in reconciling with a member of my family.):

_____

7. The good news for me in this step and these passages (Jesus has come for people like Zacchaeus and me—sinners who need Him.):

_____

CHAPTER 9

MAKING AMENDS

▼

Step Nine:

I make amends with the people I have hurt, except when to do so might bring harm to them or others.

Now, more than twenty years after her childhood, Rita took the initiative to try to mend broken family relationships. She felt an urgency about it. Time seemed to be running out. Her parents were aging, and she didn't want to spend the rest of her life with so many unresolved matters. She had many friends who had regretted not saying something to their parents before their deaths.

Since she was angry with both of her parents, she needed to deal with both.

She had been debating about going back home for years. "Why do I want to do this? Isn't it best to leave all this as it is? Why dig up stuff from the past? it won't do anyone any good."

But now her decision was clear and firm. It would be important for her own health, primarily, and she was confident that the whole family would benefit from her breaking the ice.

For as far back as she could remember, her family was not very communicative. Holiday gatherings were always the same—boring and predictable. The same old stories were told over and over again. The whole family seemed to be walking on eggshells. No one wanted to share any feelings for fear that the "dam would burst" and overwhelm them all.

Rita left each of these gatherings with greater frustration than before. "I can't take these family things anymore," she said to her husband, John. "Our family is sick. We don't even know how to communicate with each other."

So with all that experience behind her, Rita decided to talk about the past with her family. She knew the risk involved. If she opened this "can of worms," she could be ostracized by the family. But she had hope. She faithfully expected something better to come from this "leap".

She went first of all to her older sister. "Sarah, I need your help. I am going back to Mama and Daddy. I'm going to talk with them about what happened to me when I was at home. I need your help. Will you please help me?"

As they talked, Rita was surprised to discover that Sarah had resolved many of these important feelings and issues in her own life. Sarah had kept her journey private. They spent two hours together recalling both the chaotic and the good times they had growing up. They were honest in their assessment: The family had strengths and weaknesses, like all families.

But where to go from here? Rita's sister had chosen not to confront her father about his abuse. She had chosen not to approach her mother about her neglect and silence.

Rita, on the other hand, was convinced she had to deal with them. She asked for Sarah's support. After much thought, her sister agreed to join her as she went to make amends with their parents.

How about You?

To the best of your ability, describe below what holds you back from mending the broken relationships in your life:
____ I fear rejection.
____ I am anxious about the response.
____ I am embarrassed about the issues I will need to raise.
____ It's not worth it.
____ It's no big deal. I really don't need to go.

To the best of your ability, describe the benefits you get from keeping your distance from this person(s):
____ It feels safer to keep things as they are.
____ I'm so used to living this way, changing my relationship with this person would be too hard to do.
____ It's become a game to keep dancing around each other; I don't know how to stop the game.
____ I don't know.

To help you get started in taking Step Nine, think about the list you made in Step Eight. Of this list, which three have you hurt the most?

1. Name: _____

 How was the relationship hurt?_____

 _____

 _____

Verbal amend (What will you say?):

_____

_____

_____

Is any other amend necessary (For instance, A letter; payment for something stolen; a personal visit)?

_____ Yes   _____ No

If yes, what should it be? _____

_____

When will you do this step (specific time and date)?

_____

Where will you do this step (specific place)?

_____

Anything else you need to do to prepare for this meeting:

_____

2. Name: _____

How was the relationship hurt?_____

_____

_____

Verbal amend (What will you say?):

_____

_____

_____

Is any other amend necessary (For instance, A letter; payment for something stolen; a personal visit)?

_____ Yes   _____ No

If yes, what should it be? _____

_____

When will you do this step (specific time and date)?

_____

Where will you do this step (specific place)?

_____

Anything else you need to do to prepare for this meeting:

_____

3. Name: _____

How was the relationship hurt? _____

_____

_____

Verbal amend (What will you say?):

_____

_____

_____

Is any other amend necessary (For instance, A letter; payment for something stolen; a personal visit)?

____ Yes   ____ No

If yes, what should it be? _____

_____

When will you do this step (specific time and date)?

_____

Where will you do this step (specific place)?

_____

Anything else you need to do to prepare for this meeting:

_____

The Bible tells the story of one son who had the courage to return to his home to make amends to his father.

The Prodigal Son

Once there was a man who had two sons. The younger one said to his father, "Father, give me my share of the property that will come to me in my inheritance." So the father divided up his property between the two sons. Before very long, the younger son collected all his belongings and went off to a foreign land, where he squandered his wealth in wild living.

When he had run through all his money, a terrible famine arose, and he began to feel the pinch. Then he went and hired himself out to one of the citizens of that country, who sent him out into the fields to feed the pigs. He got to the point of longing to stuff himself with pig food, but not a person would offer him anything.

Then he came to his senses and cried aloud, "Dozens of my father's hired men have more food than they can eat, and here I am dying of hunger!" I will get up and go back to my father and I will say to him, "Father, I have done wrong in the sight of heaven and in your eyes. I don't deserve to be called your son any more. Please take me on as one of your hired men."

So he got up and went to his father. But while he was still some distance off, his father saw him, and his heart went out to him, and he ran and fell and kissed him on his neck. But his son said, "Father, I have done wrong in the sight of heaven and in your eyes. I don't deserve to be called your son anymore."

"Hurry," called out his father to the servants. "Get the best clothes and put them on him! Put a ring on his finger and shoes on his feet. Get that calf we've fattened and kill it, and we will have a feast and a celebration! For this is my son. I thought he was dead, and he's alive again. I thought I had lost him and he's found!" And they began to get the festivities going (based on Luke 15:11–24).

1. In this story:
____ I am like the son, returning to ask forgiveness and to make amends.
____ I am like the father, waiting for someone to return to me to make amends.
____ I can't relate to this story.
____ I see God the Father waiting for me to come back home to Him.

____

2. The main thing I get out of this story right now is
____ Don't ask for your inheritance when you are young.
____ Jesus is like the father.
____ How the father forgave the son and was waiting for him to return.
____ I want to go "home" to get things straightened out.

____

3. The hardest thing about going to make amends for me is
____ making up my mind whether I should go.
____ making the first move to go.
____ going.

4. For just a few moments, pretend you are the son who returns home after wasting his inheritance. What are your feelings as you are walking toward your home and see your father stepping out to meet you?

_____

_____

5. Talk with your group or write about the most important person that you need to make amends with. What is your plan for making amends?

_____

_____

_____

_____

Rita knew that taking the initiative to deal with her parents involved some serious physical risks. Their mother had a heart condition. By dealing with her anger toward her mother, she could possibly trigger a massive heart failure. Was it best to leave well enough alone and avoid saying what she really felt?

Hours of prayer and agonizing went into Rita's choice. She knew her family would live in denial forever if she did not take the initiative to clear the air. She had worked through most of her anger so that she didn't need to go to her mother to "blow her away." Rita felt she had found a healthy balance between compassion for her mother and appropriate anger.

It was a beautiful fall day when Rita and her sister decided to make the drive to the family farm. As they drove the two hundred miles, Rita rehearsed in her mind how she might begin the conversation. Starting would be the hardest. She was thankful for John and her group. They were behind her. They were praying for her. They were supportive of her choice to face her family. She also was well grounded in Scripture.

What the Bible Says about Step Nine

Choose one passage from the selections given and read it each day during the next week. Think about how the passage might apply to you as you reflect on the choices given. As a final comment, write your own personal application of the passage to your life.

1. Jesus is talking to His heavenly Father when He says, "**I pray that all of them may be one, Father, just as You are in Me and I am in You. May they also be in Us so that the world may believe that You have sent Me**" (based on John 17:21).

____ I know that God wants me to be one (united) with my family and friends.
____ I believe that Jesus has prayed that we would all be one.
____ I want to be united with my family and friends.
____ I ask God to help me do this step.

____ _____
____ _____
____ _____

2. Paul in his letter to the Ephesians wrote about reconciliation. He described how Jesus has made two separated parties into one. Jesus has done the uniting, he says, and broken down the barrier between them:

But now, in Christ Jesus, you who once were far away have been brought near through the blood of Christ. For He Himself is our peace, who has made the two one and has destroyed the barrier, the dividing wall of hostility, by abolishing in His flesh the law with its commandments and regulations. His purpose was to create in Himself one new man out of the two, thus making peace, and in this one body to reconcile both of them to God through the cross, by which He put to death their hostility. He came and preached peace to you who were far away and peace to those who were near. For through Him we both have access to the Father by one Spirit. Consequently, you are no longer foreigners and aliens, but fellow citizens with God's people and members of God's household, built on the foundation of the apostles and prophets, with Christ Jesus Himself as the chief cornerstone. In Him the whole building is joined together and rises to become a holy temple in the Lord. And in Him you, too, are being built together to become a dwelling in which God lives by His Spirit (based on Eph. 2:13–22).

____ God has taken the initiative in calling me back into a relationship with Himself. I am no longer a foreigner or alien. I am a citizen of heaven.
____ Jesus has broken down the wall between me and my "brother."

___ He has taken away the hostility and replaced it with His peace.

___ I want to go share that peace with my "brother."

___ _____

3. Paul writes about our right, privilege, and call to be reconcilers. Paul and Jesus make reconciliation one of the highest priorities:

> **Therefore, if anyone is in Christ, he is a new creation; the old has gone, the new has come! All this is from God, who reconciled us to Himself through Christ and gave us the ministry of reconciliation that God was reconciling the world to Himself in Christ, not counting men's sins against them. And He has committed to us the message of reconciliation. We are therefore Christ's ambassadors, as though God were making His appeal through us. We implore you on Christ's behalf: Be reconciled to God** (based on 2 Cor. 5:17–20).

___ God has made me a new creation by calling me into a relationship with Himself.

___ He has now given me the privilege of being a friend-maker for Him.

___ He is appealing to others through me, urging them to be reconciled to God.

___ I want to be His representative in all of my relationships.

___ _____

Rita had worked through these Scriptures before she drove back to the farm. She had no expectations from her mother or dad. She was going there to express her feelings and to apologize for her behavior. She had a fantasy about the outcome of this meeting. That fantasy, of course, had a happy ending, but people in her group warned her to be realistic and to be prepared for anything. The individuals in the group had a variety of experiences with this step.

Some of them had learned the hard way that often those we come to share with are not prepared for this meeting. They are sometimes in shock and denial. They don't know how to respond.

Rita Takes Step Nine

When Rita and her sister arrived at the farm, their father was out in the fields. Her mother, now in her mid-seventies, gray, and looking tired as ever, was there to meet them at the front door.

This was hard for Rita. The family had been good at keeping secrets. For all these years, all family members had learned how to dance around what was really important. No one could be honest. No one shared feelings.

The small talk went on for as long as Rita could stand it. Then she burst into tears. "Mama, I've got to talk with you. I need your help. I'm afraid to bring this up . . ." she hesitated, "but I need to do it."

Mama sat down at the kitchen table in her "spot." She waited quietly and patiently for Rita to continue.

"Mama, I've got to know if you know what happened to me. I have to know why you didn't protect me! I am so angry at you. You let me down. Couldn't you do anything? Couldn't you stop Dad from calling me those awful names?"

Rita wanted to say so much more, but she realized that she had said enough. The silence was profound.

Mama stared out into the barren prairie that surrounded the old farmstead. She looked as if she wanted to say something, but held back, for fear that once she began, she would never be able to stop.

Rita waited and waited. She realized that her mother had learned to numb herself when painful things came up. For the first time, Rita understood how her mother had tolerated all that happened. She could see here, in front of her, with her own eyes, a woman who had suffered greatly and helplessly. When there was pain, her mother deliberately numbed herself, shifted into neutral, and became passive.

Mama had grown up in a family that was very private, Rita knew. No one talked about anything serious. Silence was best. In fact it was admirable to be silent. At relatives' funerals, Rita could not remember any of her mother's relatives crying at the loss of their brother and sister. Now, here was Mama, living a life of "solitary confinement." She didn't know that life could be so rich if she could simply share herself more openly.

Rita got up slowly, walked over, stood behind Mama, and gently put her arms around her neck. Tears rolled down as she said, "Mama, I love you. I came here today to let you know that I love you, and I ask you to forgive me for being so angry with you all these years. I'm so sorry, Mama. I'm truly sorry."

Rita's sister came to the other side of Mama. She broke down, cried, and laid her head on Mama's shoulder. "Oh, Mama, I feel so bad about what's happened in our life. I feel so sorry for you," she said.

"No need, my child. No need for that," Mama said as she continued to look straight out into the prairie. "I'm okay. Things are getting better for us. Your daddy's been really good to me, and he's getting better. You gotta believe me. He's been doing some changin'. You'll see."

Rita and her sister didn't know that their father had been going to A.A. They had seen some differences in him the last two times they had been with him, but they didn't know how to account for them or whether they were permanent. "He'll be glad to see you," Mama said. "I expect him back any minute."

Rita and her sister were anxious about his return. They didn't know what to expect. While they waited, Rita told Mama about what she had been going through with John and how she hoped this kind of talk would make a difference in their relationship. Mama said she understood.

Rita's heart almost stopped beating as her father came through the back door. She could tell by her first look into his eyes that something had changed in him. Instead of greeting Rita and Sarah in his usual loud, nervous, superficial way, he quietly and gently embraced them one by one and whispered in their ears. "I'm so glad to see you. So glad you're here."

"Rita," he said, "I've been meanin' to get up there to see you. Would you mind if we go for a short walk?"

Rita nodded, and together they walked out onto the porch and then into the yard. As they walked across Rita's old "baseball field," tears began to run down his cheeks. Not once in her life could Rita remember seeing tears in her dad's eyes. Today, all that was different. And Rita was ready to cry.

She had written two letters to her parents, hinting that she might come to talk about a few things with them. Her dad picked up on those hints and apparently decided to take the lead.

"I've been meaning to talk with you, Rita. I've been thinking about doing it for a long time. But what I want to talk with you about is hard for me."

As best Rita could gather, her father grew up in an environment where the men could best be characterized as hard working, resilient, strong, and powerful. Never did they reveal their true feelings. Seldom did they express any tenderness or gentleness. The manly way was the stern way.

Years ago, Rita was really mad about that. Now, she had compassion. She knew that she now had the opportunity to break the pattern and develop something new and different for her children and their children's children. What was happening in her life right at this moment was another major step in the development of that new family order.

Her father continued, "I know I was a terrible daddy for you, Rita." He hesitated, not sure what to say next. "I just wish there would be a way to undo some of the things that I did to you. I wish I could remake the past."

Rita's dad was nervously shifting his weight from one leg to another. He looked straight out toward the setting sun in the west and then down at the ground. He looked like a sixth-grade boy who was embarrassed because he had been caught smoking in a locker room.

"I've thought about those things over and over, and I'm telling you I'm sorry. I'm so sorry for what I did to hurt you and your sister.'' For years he had been living in remorse. Rita's coming opened the door for him to say all this.

As he finished his sentence, he reached his arms out to Rita. He pulled her to him and began to weep.

"I'm so sorry, my little darling. I'm so sorry."

Rita couldn't believe what she was hearing. Most of her adult life she had longed to hear those words. She had prayed to hear them. Many times she had dreamed about a scene like this. And now that she was hearing them, she didn't know what to do or say. It felt so good to be in her father's arms. She stood in silence thinking, about how this daddy—this loving daddy—was the daddy of her dreams—a great man, a tender man, a strong man. This was the person that was her real dad.

Every moment made Rita healthier and stronger. She felt she was becoming a new person, right then and there. The plug on all the anger that she had stored up against her father had been pulled and was draining the anger away.

With all her strength, Rita hugged him back and finally found a few words to express her joy. "Daddy, I'm so proud of you. Thank you for saying what you said. I love you, Daddy. You are a courageous man. Thank you for this day."

Rita's initiative in wanting to take this ninth step opened the door for all these good things to happen.

One year after this encounter Rita's father died.

Unfortunately all ninth-step encounters are not this positive. Most people who go to make amends are rejected in one form or another. Many times the people they go to deny that anything has taken place. Many have forgotten. Many choose to keep things as they are.

That's why it is best to go back without expecting anything in return. That's a great definition for love—to give without expecting anything back. To go to make amends is to go in love. This kind of love will not be disappointed.

Jim, a group participant, went into the ministry after getting an undergraduate degree in engineering. He had been a volunteer for his church for five years. He knew God was calling him to full-time ministry.

To make a long story short, his father resented Jim's doing this. He was clear in stating why he disapproved. Jim felt torn and knew that following what he perceived to be God's call would deeply affect his relationship with his father.

He chose to enter ministry and has been there for fifteen years. Much tension has plagued his relationship with his father as a consequence. For five years, Jim had been struggling with going back to his dad to talk this through. Finally, last year, he did it.

Before he could finish his first sentence, his father shut him down. He would not discuss it. He wanted nothing to do with trying to reconcile. Although nothing clearly positive has come about yet, Jim is confident that seeds have been planted. He feels good because he has done his part to make amends.

Doing Step Nine

I make amends with the people I have hurt, except when to do so might bring harm to them or others.

Often my advice to people I counsel spiritually is, ''You gotta do it now. You can't wait any longer.''

Recently a high school student was called out of class by the principal. Someone from the family was waiting in the office. As the student entered, he knew something serious had happened. He was right. His father had been killed suddenly in a car accident a few hours before. The son was overwhelmed. He loved his father dearly. Both father and son were very well-known and liked in the school.

In no time the news spread through the school. An unusual thing happened in every break between classes for the rest of that day. At each break, kids were lined up at every available telephone, calling their dads to let them know they loved them.

Step Nine reminds us of the urgency in going to people to express our love and concern. Don't hesitate. The importance of being reunited with others cannot be overemphasized. The need is indescribable. Nothing can surpass the wonderful feelings of having restored relationships, of being reconciled.

As people involved in the Twelve-Step process, our part is to go to the people with whom we need to restore a relationship. We go to express our feelings, our apologies, our sorrow about the broken relationship. Sometimes we need to go to ask forgiveness. We always need to forgive them for what they have done (or not done) to us before we go.

We go without expecting anything in return from the other persons. Their response is their response—we cannot control it. It would be best if they accept your apology. But they may not. You cannot do anything about that. They may reject you. That is the risk you will take. However, you will be at peace inside because you did what you could to improve the relationship.

Step Nine gives us an excuse to go to others. Usually, our strongest and best relationships are the ones that have had a reconciliation, ones where the two parties have come back together after a time of disagreement. Use this ninth step to get closer to the people from whom you have been separated.

Making Step Nine My Own

This section provides you with a format for integrating your feelings, your responses to questions, and what you learned from this step, from the Scriptures, and in your group meetings.

Date, day, and time of your writings:

_____

1. At this point in my life, the major area that I am working on (For instance, actually going to make amends; I have thought about doing this for a long time; now is the time.):

_____

_____

2. Major insights I was given into my life through this step (There is great joy in restoring a relationship. I want this joy.):

_____

_____

_____

_____

3. The scriptural passage that spoke to me most clearly in this step (Jesus has broken down the wall that divided us.):

_____

The one word that has been most important to me in this chapter (Ambassador—I am an ambassador for God.):

_____

_____

4. The major discovery about Jesus Christ that I was given in this step (Jesus' prayer and longing for us to be one):

_____

_____

5. The strongest feeling I have as I have worked this step (a great desire to want to go do this step, a feeling of excitement and adventure):

_____

6. The action I feel called to take as a result of working this step (Go to it.):

_____

7. The good news for me in this step and these passages (Joy will come from my being obedient.):

_____

CHAPTER 10

DAILY

REVIEW

▼

Step Ten:

Each day I do a review of

myself and my activities.

When I am wrong, I quickly

admit it. When I am right,

I thank God for the guidance.

I went to parochial schools for grade school and high school. I'll never forget the hard oak desks and beautifully polished oak floors. Specifically, I remember the blackboards in our classrooms.

In grade school, the blackboards were used frequently. By the end of the day, the boards were chalky white. One of the students stayed after school to clean the boards with wet rags. As the rest of us left school for the day, we couldn't help but notice how whitened the blackboards had become. Sometimes students were ''selected'' to clean the boards because of their behavior. (I was often selected. I'll never forget the smell and feel of those ''holy'' rags. I hated this project.)

When we returned to school in the morning, the boards were clean. I felt I could start a new day with a clean slate. As an adult, I need simple reminders like this.

It is important for us to clean our personal boards every day. Our hearts and minds need a daily cleansing, just as our bodies do.

If I want to live peacefully with freedom from guilt, I need to spend a few minutes at the end of each day looking over what the day has been like for me. Then I can let go of this day, close the door on it, and be ready to open the door to a new and fresh day.

What about You?

You may think that taking a daily review or doing a daily inventory is a complicated task, but it really is very simple: I simply spend the last few minutes of each day reflecting on what the day was like. I follow the pattern laid out below. (A more detailed exercise is on page 153).

1. Recall in sequence the most important people that you have been with or spoken with throughout the day.

149

2. Ask God to forgive you if you have been at fault in any of these events.
3. Forgive others if they were at fault in these events.
4. If you need to make amends in any of these situations, do so.
5. Thank God for the good things that have happened today and the guidance that He has given.
6. Close the door to the day as best you can. Forgive and forget. Give thanks for another day of life. I sometimes read the Serenity Prayer (see page 156).

A number of scriptural passages reinforce the need to do this daily review. The psalmist says, **"Search me, O God, and know my heart . . . lead me"** (Ps. 139:23–24). He also says, Lord, **"remember how short my time is"** (Ps. 89:47). A day is a lifetime. Our lifetime is brief. Today is all we have. One day at a time, we carefully live out the moments given to us.

> A businessman was permitted to have one wish come true. After some thought he wished for a newspaper dated two years into the future. Miraculously the paper appeared in his hands. Turning to the stock reports, he made careful notes on the stocks that had shown unusual growth. He would certainly make a fortune.
>
> Then out of curiosity he looked through the paper and, scanning the obituary column, found his name in it. He had suffered a heart attack, and his funeral arrangements were spelled out in detail there before him.
>
> In His wisdom God hides the future from us. He wants us to live one day at a time. He wishes us to make today count. (Author Unknown)

At the end of the day I often use what I call the "tombstone test." If I were to die today, what would my family write on my tombstone? If I were to die today, what message would I like to have on my tombstone? I want to live each day as if it is my last.

Paul says, **"Judge yourselves soberly. . . . use your gifts. . . . have a profound respect for each other. . . . and be reconciled"** (based on Rom. 12:3–13). In Galatians he says, **"Let each one examine his own work"** (6:4). And in 1 John 1:8—2:2 we are given the reminder that if we acknowledge our sin and confess it, Jesus Christ will forgive us.

Doing a daily review or "inventory" is a matter of habit. It is a way of life. It is a great way to use the natural rhythm and cycle of daily life to remind us of the need to stay close to God, ourselves, and others. Step Ten helps prevent the "stockpiling" of anxiety, sin, and broken relationships. If we did Step Ten alone, without any of the other steps, it would bring renewal, vitality, and stability to our lives.

Let's look at what the Bible says about taking a review of ourselves, admitting when we are wrong and thanking God when we are right.

What the Bible Says about Step Ten

1. Do Not Think of Yourself More Highly Than You Ought

Paul wrote his letter to the Romans urging them to do an honest assessment of both their gifts and weaknesses. Paul wanted people to know and use their gifts. His writings on this subject had a sense of urgency about them. The following passage emphasizes the need for a daily review.

> **For by the grace given me I say to every one of you: Do not think of yourself more highly than you ought, but rather think of yourself with sober judgment, in accordance with the measure of faith God has given you. Just as each of us has one body with many members, and these members do not all have the same function, so in Christ we who are many form one body, and each member belongs to all the others. We have different gifts, according to the grace given us** (based on Rom. 12:3–6).

____ It is important for me to assess myself and my behavior realistically.

____ I need to know more about my place in the "body".

____ I want to do a daily review to assess whether I am making the best use of my time and gifts.

____ I want to grow in my respect for others in the body who have different gifts.

2. Test Your Own Actions

Paul wrote a letter to his Galatian friends to underscore the need for each person to review his or her own behavior, not anyone else's. **"Each one should test his own actions. Then he can take pride in himself, without comparing himself to somebody else"** (based on Gal. 6:4).

____ I am responsible for my own behavior and the assessment of that behavior.

____ I need not be concerned with what others do or what they think of me.

____ I sometimes compare myself to others.

3. Put Off Falsehood

To help the early Christians live fulfilling lives together, Paul gave the following practical advice to the Ephesians. These are great words for doing the tenth step.

> **Now your attitudes and thoughts must all be constantly changing for the better with each passing day. Every day, put on the new self, the new nature that God has given to you. Stop lying to each other; tell the truth, for we are all parts of each other and when we lie to each other we are hurting ourselves. Don't let the sun set on your anger. Deal with it. Get it resolved. Be reconciled before the end of the day or you will be giving the devil a mighty foothold. If anyone is stealing, that person must stop and begin using his or her gifts for honest work so he or she can give to others in need. Don't use bad language. Say only what is good and helpful to those you are talking to and what will give them a blessing. Don't cause the Holy Spirit sorrow by the way you live. He is the one who seals your salvation until the day of your arrival in heaven. Stop being mean, bad-tempered, and angry. Quarreling, harsh words, and dislike of others should have no place in your lives. Instead, be kind to each other, tender-hearted, forgiving one another, just as God has forgiven you because you belong to Christ Jesus** (based on Eph. 4:23–32).

____ This list makes a lot of sense to me. The part that especially speaks to me right now is_____

_____

_____

____ I need God's help to make the changes this passage suggests.

____ I want to use this passage for my daily review.

____ I'm not ready to do any of this stuff yet.

Now that I have read these passages, the idea of doing a daily review of myself and my activities seems

____ tedious. I really don't have the time for it.

____ terrific. I've done it for years. It's the only way to live.

____ exciting, but I don't know how to do it.

____ to be a great idea, but I know myself well enough to know I'll never do it.

____ like something I want to develop.

When I am wrong, I generally

____ deny it.

____ avoid it.

_____ pretend it didn't happen.
_____ admit it.
_____ find someone else to blame.
_____ ask forgiveness.

Doing Step Ten

Each day I do a review of myself and my activities. When I am wrong, I quickly admit it. When I am right, I thank God for the guidance.

A Daily Inventory

In just a few minutes at the end of each day, you can do the daily inventory below. Use the form to help you get started. When we do a daily review, four simple and basic principles given to us by Jesus are the ultimate test of whether we are living a rich and full life. These are some of the greatest passages from the Bible. All daily reviews must include these principles.

Jesus said you must:

1. **"Love the LORD your God with all your heart, with all your soul, and with all your mind"** (Matt. 22:37)
2. **"Love your neighbor as yourself"** (Matt. 22:39)
3. **"Love your enemies"** and
4. **"Pray for those who . . . persecute you"** (Matt. 5:44)

One way to do a daily review is to look at these four passages and simply ask yourself, Have I lived by each of these principles today?

Another way to do a daily review is to look at what Paul has written in two of his letters. Both of these are great daily review resources.

Paul wrote a "love letter" to the Corinthians. You've probably heard it read at weddings. Now you can use it for a daily review of your life.
_____ Today, have I been patient?
_____ Today, have I been kind?
_____ Today, have I been jealous?
_____ Today, have I been boastful or conceited?
_____ Today, have I been rude or selfish?
_____ Today, have I taken offense or been resentful?
_____ Today, have I taken pleasure in other people's sins or misfortunes?
_____ Today, have I delighted in the truth?
_____ Today, did I trust God and others?

_____ Today, did I express hope?
_____ Today, did I endure what came my way?
_____ Today, did I love without conditions?

(based on 1 Cor. 13:4–8)

In his letter to the Galatians, Paul listed what he called the "fruit of the Spirit" (5:22–23). These "fruits" were the evidence that a person was a Christian. Use these daily to evaluate your life.
The fruits of the Holy Spirit...
_____ Today, have I been loving?
_____ Today, have I been filled with joy?
_____ Today, have I been at peace?
_____ Today, have I been patient?
_____ Today, have I been kind?
_____ Today, have I demonstrated goodness?
_____ Today, have I been trustful?
_____ Today, have I been gentle?
_____ Today, have I demonstrated self-control?

No one person is capable of having or doing all of these in his or her own power. We all need Jesus Christ to come into our lives and give us hearts that will be able to do all these important things. When we receive Jesus Christ, He gives us the ability to do what He asks of us. He wouldn't ask us to do something that we're not capable of doing with Him living inside of us. He, living in us, gives us the ability to love, to pray, and to give of ourselves.

As our relationship with Jesus grows, our ability to love also grows. The more we get to know His love for us, the more we can love other people around us, even if they don't love us in return.

In light of the passages from the Bible on the previous pages, use the form below to help you with your daily review.

1. Recall in sequence the most important people that you have been with or spoken with throughout this day.

The person _____

The event _____

_____

The person _____

The event _____

_____

The person _____

The event _____

_____

The person _____

The event _____

_____

2. Ask God to forgive you if you have been at fault in any of these events.

3. Forgive others if they were at fault in these events.

4. If you need to make amends in any of these situations, do so.

Person _____

I will make amends right now or make a plan to do so tomorrow.

____ Yes ____ No

Person _____

I will make amends right now or make a plan to do so tomorrow.

____ Yes ____ No

Person _____

I will make amends right now or make a plan to do so tomorrow.

____ Yes ____ No

Person _____

I will make amends right now or make a plan to do so tomorrow.

____ Yes ____ No

5. Thank God for the good things that have happened today and the guidance that He has given.

Lord, I thank you for _____

Lord, I thank you for _____

Lord, I thank you for _____

Lord, I thank you for _____

6. Close the door to the day. Forgive and forget. Give thanks for another day of life. Read the Serenity Prayer.

> God,
> grant me the serenity to accept the things I cannot change,
> courage to change the things I can
> and wisdom to know the difference,
> living one day at a time,
> enjoying one moment at a time,
> accepting hardship as a pathway to peace
> taking as Jesus did, this sinful world as it is,
> not as I would have it,
> trusting that You will make all things right
> as I surrender to Your will,
> so that I may be reasonably happy in this life
> and supremely happy with You forever in the next.

Making Step Ten My Own

This section provides you with a format for integrating your feelings, responses to questions, and what you learned from this step, the Scriptures, and your group meetings.

Date, day, and time of your writings:

_____

1. At this point in my life, the major area that I am working on (For instance, The challenge of doing a daily review. I know I need it. I know it will take some effort on my part to do it.):

_____

_____

2. Major insights I was given into my life through this step (the importance of checking in with myself and God each day):

_____

_____

_____

_____

3. The scriptural passage that spoke to me most clearly in this step (Do not let the sun set on my anger.):

_____

The one word that has been most important to me in this chapter (Obedience—not only listening to God's word but acting on it):

_____

_____

4. The major discovery about Jesus Christ that I was given in this step (Jesus is faithful; If I confess my sins, he will be faithful in forgiving me.):

_____

_____

5. My strongest feeling as I have worked this step (Hope—I feel hopeful about what this daily review will do for me.):

_____

6. The action I feel called to take as a result of working this step (to do a daily review):

_____

7. The good news for me in this step and these passages (the joy that comes from being in touch with myself, God, and others each day):

_____

CHAPTER 11

MY MOST IMPORTANT DAILY APPOINTMENT

▼

Step Eleven:

To keep growing in my relationship with Jesus Christ, I spend time each day praying and reading the Bible. I will gather with others who do the same. I ask Jesus for guidance and the power to do what He wants me to do.

itting in my office for about the tenth time was a very handsome twenty-nine-year-old man. All the young women in the area "noticed" him and talked about him. He was one of the most unusual young persons I had known. When he talked, his words had integrity. He had been raised in a healthy, loving family. Though his father was a driven financier, Joe seemed to survive with the minimal amount of time his dad gave him.

As we explored the areas of his life that Joe felt needed attention, we seldom found any problem or issue that Joe had not openly identified and was not already dealing with.

"I want more than anything else to live my life for Jesus Christ. He has loved me so much, the least I can do in response is give Him my life," Joe said. When he talked like that, he didn't sound like a weirdo or Jesus freak. He was for real.

"I could spend the rest of my life looking at myself. I don't want that. I want to look at Jesus. I want to look at others. I want my life to count for something. I think the way it will count for something is if I use my gifts in serving others." He said all this emphatically. He was sincere.

He wasn't denying his problems and issues; he simply wanted to put them in perspective and move ahead with his life.

"I don't want to get stuck on myself. I truly want to be a disciple of Christ. What does it mean to be a disciple in the late twentieth century?" he asked.

Joe, I thought, was a very mature person for his age. He had already outgrown the need to be "successful" or accumulate material things. His life was focused on all the right things.

Joe had gone through the Twelve-Step process many times in various forms. He had "worked" the steps and grown immensely. He could relate very well to others and the kids he worked with in his church.

Because he had done so much work with the steps, he did not live his life in compartments. He was the same person on Monday as he was on Sunday. He was a congruent person: His words, his feelings, and his attitude matched his behavior.

"It's what the eleventh step teaches that is making me feel so healthy," he said. "This step is the single most important step I can do for myself. I spend the first time of the day in prayer and reading the Bible. Usually that's about an hour. It has become the most important hour in my day."

Joe was at peace. He did not work at impressing. He was confident and yet knew his limitations. "I know I'm young," he said, "but I think I'm ready to keep moving toward the things that God wants me to do.

"And I study the Bible," he continued. "I carry a verse from the Bible with me every day. I read it often. I pray about it. When it's appropriate, I share that verse with one of my friends at work or socially.

"Each week, I get together with a small group of guys from my church. We talk about what's going in our lives. We use these steps to help us focus. And we pray for each other," he said. "I've been doing this ever since I was fifteen. I couldn't live without my brothers and sisters. I need their support."

Joe stands on a solid foundation. He is ready to do whatever God wants him to do. He is beyond "recovery" and into the great things that life has to offer.

Joe takes Step Eleven each day. He practices the four parts of this step:

- Keep a daily appointment with God
- Read the Bible
- Gather with others who pray and read the Bible
- Ask Jesus for power to do what he wants us to do.

Understanding the clear and simple characteristics of Step Eleven is easy. *Doing* them is quite another thing. Step Eleven reminds us that if we want a close relationship with Jesus Christ, we will need to spend time with Him each day. Time in prayer and reading the Bible is essential to intimacy with God.

Gathering with others to share our lives, experiences, and insights is also essential to maintaining a good relationship with Jesus Christ. The world is trying to convince us that spiritual and eternal things don't really count. We need to be with other Christians who remind us that God is alive and real.

"What my friends do for me is alert me to the power that the world has," Joe said. "Without my Christian friends, I could easily be convinced that you find the good life in having new cars, clothes, and houses. I thank God that I'm growing out of that phase."

Part of our daily prayer and reading is to seek the guidance that Jesus gives to us moment by moment and day by day. Prayer prepares us to receive His guidance. It alerts us to His presence. It shapes our character.

Another part of our daily prayer and reading is to be open to the power that Jesus will give us. Jesus instructed His disciples to wait in Jerusalem until they received the Holy Spirit and power. In much the same way, I believe, Jesus wants us to ''wait'' until he fills us with His Holy Spirit—day by day.

The Bible has a lot to say about the importance of prayer.

What the Bible Says about Step Eleven

Read the following short passages several times each day this week:

> Ask and you will receive; seek, and you will find; knock, and the door will be opened to you. The one who asks will receive, and anyone who seeks will find, and the door will be opened to the person who knocks.
>
> There is no need to worry. If there is anything you need, pray for it, asking God for it with prayer and thanksgiving, and that peace of God which is so much greater than we can understand will guard your hearts and minds in Christ Jesus.
>
> Pray constantly.
>
> Very early, long before daylight, Jesus got up and left the house. He went out to a lonely place, where He prayed.
>
> The Spirit comes to help us pray, weak as we are. For we don't know how to pray. The Spirit pleads with God for us in groans that words cannot express.
>
> . . . for where two or three meet in My name, I will be there with them. (based on Matt. 7:7–9; Phil. 4:6–7; 1 Thess. 5:17; Luke 4:42; Rom. 8:26; Matt. 18:20)

Think about how you spend your time every day. What is the least important thing you do?

How would you like to spend your time?

Are you wasting time?

These brief passages are not the only passages in the Bible that talk about the importance of prayer and Bible study. Select a passage from the following scriptures to read each day this week. Think about the passage by checking the statements below that reflect how you feel. Then write your own personal application of the passage as a final comment.

1. Matthew 4:4—Jesus was led into the desert by the Spirit. There He was tempted by the devil in three ways. After forty days of fasting, when Satan

tempted Jesus to make bread out of stones, Jesus answered, **"It is written, 'Man shall not live by bread alone, but by every word that proceeds from the mouth of God'"** (based on v. 4).

____ I'm convinced I need spiritual nourishment as well as physical nourishment each day.

____ I will set time aside each day for this.

____ I am ready to head into the desert to hear God's voice more clearly.

____ I have a long way to go before I can really do this step.

____ _____

____ _____

____ _____

2. Matthew 6:5–13—Jesus gave His disciples clear, specific, and practical teaching on prayer. Jesus said:

> **And when you pray, you shall not be like the hypocrites. For they love to pray standing in the synagogues and on the corners of the streets, that they may be seen by men. Assuredly, I say to you, they have their reward. But you, when you pray, go into your room, and when you have shut your door, pray to your Father who is in the secret place; and your Father who sees in secret will reward you openly. But when you pray, do not use vain repetitions as the heathen do. For they think they will be heard for their many words . . . do not be like them. For your Father knows the things you have need of before you ask Him. In this manner, therefore, pray:**

> > **Our Father in heaven,**
> > **Hallowed be Your name.**
> > **Your kingdom come.**
> > **Your will be done**
> > **On earth as it is in heaven.**
> > **Give us this day our daily bread.**
> > **And forgive us our debts,**
> > **As we forgive our debtors.**
> > **And do not lead us into temptation,**
> > **But deliver us from the evil one. . . .**

> **For if you forgive men their trespasses, your heavenly Father will also forgive you.** (Matt. 6:14)

____ God, help me to trust that You see what is done in secret and You will hear my prayer.

___ God, please give me the courage to pray this way.
___ Lord Jesus, please help me to do this prayer.

___ _____

___ _____

___ _____

3. Matthew 18:8–20—This is one of Jesus' greatest and strongest promises to the Church: **"Whatever you bind on earth will be bound in heaven, and whatever you loose on earth will be loosed in heaven. Again I say to you that if two of you agree on earth concerning anything that they ask, it will be done for them by My Father in heaven. For where two or three are gathered together in My name, I am there in the midst of them"** (vv. 18–20).
___ Jesus, please give me "two or three" others that I can pray with so that together we can exercise your power on earth.
___ I'm not ready to pray like this.
___ I'm ready to pray like this, but I don't know how to get started.

___ _____

___ _____

___ _____

4. Luke 18:1–8—

> **Then Jesus told his disciples a parable to show them that they should always pray and not give up. He said: "In a certain town there was a judge who neither feared God nor cared about people. And there was a widow in that town who kept coming to him with the plea, 'Grant me justice against my adversary.'**
>
> **"For some time he refused. But finally he said to himself, 'Even though I don't fear God or care about people, yet because this widow keeps bothering me, I will see that she gets justice so that she won't eventually wear me out with her coming!'"**
>
> **"And the Lord said, 'Listen to what the unjust judge says. And will not God bring about justice for His chosen ones, who cry out to Him day and night? Will He keep putting them off? I tell you, He will see that they get justice, and quickly. However, when the Son of Man comes, will He find faith on the earth?'"** (based on vv. 1–8).

___ Lord Jesus, please grant me the persistence of the widow.
___ God, help me to trust that You will bring justice to Your chosen ones.

—— Lord Jesus, please grant me faith and persistence so that I will pray consistently and faithfully for justice to be done.

—— _____

—— _____

—— _____

5. Romans 8:26–28—As Paul was instructing the Romans to pray, he wrote:

"**The Spirit helps us in our weakness. We do not know what we ought to pray for, but the Spirit Himself intercedes for us with groans that words cannot express. And He who searches our hearts knows the mind of the Spirit, because the Spirit intercedes for the saints in accordance with God's will. And we know that in all things God works for the good of those who love him, who have been called according to his purpose** (based on vv. 26–27).

—— I am comforted to know that I do not need to be an "expert" in prayer.
—— I believe the Holy Spirit will come to intercede on my behalf.
—— This is an encouraging passage for me.

—— _____

—— _____

6. 1 Timothy 2:1–6—In some of his teaching to Timothy, Paul spells out the need and type of prayer that is to be offered:

"**I urge, then, first of all, that requests, prayers, intercession, and thanksgiving be made for everyone—for kings and all those in authority, that we may live peaceful and quiet lives in all godliness and holiness. This is good and pleases God our Savior, who wants all men to be saved and to come to a knowledge of the truth. For there is one God and one mediator between God and men, the man Christ Jesus, who gave Himself as a ransom for all people—the testimony given in its proper time**" (based on vv. 1-6).

—— Lord God, help me to pray for others.
—— The amount of time that I devote to prayer for others is the one area of my life that I feel good about.
—— Prayer for others—this is what Jesus, the one mediator between God and people, wants from me.

—— _____

___ _____

___ _____

7. Hebrews 10:24–25—The author of the Epistle to the Hebrews reminded the Hebrew Christians of their need to gather and encourage each other. This author was especially sensitive about the urgency to do so in light of the final day when Jesus would return: **"And let us consider how we may encourage one another on toward love and good deeds. Let us not give up meeting together, as some are in the habit of doing, but let us encourage one another—and all the more as you see the Day approaching"** (based on vv. 24–25).

___ I need the encouragement that comes from meeting with others who pray, follow Jesus, and read the Bible.

___ I have all the encouragement I need.

___ Jesus, I need to meet with my brothers and sisters. Help me to develop and keep this habit.

___ _____

___ _____

___ _____

After reading these passages:

1. How do you feel about praying?

___ I don't know how to do it.

___ I haven't really tried it.

___ I want to learn more about it.

___ I am undecided about prayer.

2. What phrase from the passages most likely describes where you are?

___ I ask and I know I will receive.

___ I don't worry about things. I just ask for what I need.

___ I pray constantly.

___ I gather regularly with two or three others to pray.

___ All of the above

___ None of the above

___ _____

3. How do you feel about praying twelve minutes each day (six minutes in the morning and six minutes at night)?

_____

_____

_____

4. What is the next step that you could take to make your relationship with Jesus Christ stronger?

_____

_____

_____

Doing Step Eleven

Step Eleven reminds us that there are five important things we must do if we want to keep growing stronger:

1. Keep an intimate relationship with Jesus Christ.
2. Spend time each day praying.

The most important time you can have each day is a time to meet with God. Learn to take time for God. Try an experiment. Meet with God for six minutes each morning and each night. It will become the most important twelve minutes of your day. You will experience peace and guidance that you've never had before. Make a list of people, events, and things that you will pray for every day or week.

Begin this list below.

The people I want to pray for every day:

_____   _____

_____   _____

_____   _____

_____   _____

_____   _____

_____   _____

_____   _____
_____   _____
_____   _____
_____   _____
_____   _____
_____   _____
_____   _____
_____   _____

The coming events I want to pray about each day:

_____   _____
_____   _____
_____   _____
_____   _____
_____   _____

Other people/things I want to pray for each day:

_____   _____
_____   _____
_____   _____
_____   _____
_____   _____

3. Read the Bible every day. Try reading it first thing in the morning and last thing at night. Read the passages in this book. Be sure to use a modern translation of the

Bible (like New King James, Today's English, New International, or Jerusalem). Let the Bible become your best friend.

4. Get together with others who are also growing in spirit.

5. Ask Jesus for guidance and the power to do what He wants you to do.

The focus of Step Eleven is quite clear. Nothing is more important than a daily meeting with God. We make time for everything else that seems important. Meeting with God is crucial and needs to become our first priority. Jesus said, **"Seek first the kingdom of God and His righteousness, and all these things shall be added to you"** (Matt. 6:33).

All the steps are important. Some are more pivotal than others. Step Eleven is crucial because it addresses our lifestyle and challenges us to put first things first. When our priorities are right, our lives will be coherent, "together." Fragmentation makes us frustrated and anxious because it pulls us in many directions at the same time. Daily prayer helps us focus on what's most important to God.

Occasionally, we also need prayer retreats, half days or days devoted to solitude, giving us added time to reflect on God's love.

Making Step Eleven My Own

This section provides you with a format for integrating your feelings, responses to questions, and what you learned from this step, the Scriptures, and your group meetings.

Date, day, and time of your writings:

_____

1. At this point in my life, the major area that I am working on (For instance, I need to meet with others who want to pray and read the Bible.):

_____

_____

2. Major insights I was given into my life through this step (I need to be more deliberate in my personal discipline so that I can grow spiritually.):

_____

_____

_____

_____

3. The scriptural passage that spoke to me most clearly in this step (The need to "pray constantly"—This is something I do not do.):

_____

    The one word that has been most important to me in this chapter (Meeting—Nothing is more important than my daily meeting with God.):

_____

_____

4. The major discovery about Jesus Christ that I was given in this step (There is power in the name of Jesus.):

_____

_____

5. My strongest feeling as I work this step (Encouragement; I am more eager than ever to begin and continue a daily "program" for prayer.):

_____

6. The action I feel called to take as a result of working this step (Call two friends to talk with them about getting together on a weekly basis to pray.):

_____

7. The good news for me in this step and these passages
(God has given us the ability to pray. I want to do it more.):

_____

CHAPTER 12

I WILL REACH OUT TO OTHERS

▼

Step Twelve:

I am grateful that God is changing me through these Twelve Steps. In response, I will reach out to share Christ's love by practicing these principles in all that I do.

n our training workshops I often tell the story of a man named Steve, who lived in San Francisco and had decided to end his life. All his circumstances led to despondency. For him it was simply a matter of how he would end it.

Several days went by as he thought about the ways to commit suicide. The first option he considered was to go to his office bathroom, cut his wrists, and die there. Concerned that this might be messy, he thought about another option. He would jump out of his forty-fifth-floor office window. This would be a quick way to end it all. On second thought, kind as he was, he remembered the possibility of landing on someone and taking that person's life as well.

As he pondered this some more, the best idea came to him. It would be best to jump off the bridge. Ah, that was it. That was simplest and cleanest. He put on his coat and mentally said good-bye to his office and belongings and quietly headed out to the elevator.

As the elevator moved down to the first floor, he heard a voice say, "Give life just one more chance." Conscientious as he was, he obeyed and made a decision to do just that. *If the next person I see when I get off this elevator smiles at me and greets me, that will be my sure sign that life deserves another chance,* he said to himself.

Are you the next person Steve will see?

Experience tells us that there are hundreds of "Steves" out there. Our simple smile and greeting could save their lives.

Step Twelve is about reaching out and giving ourselves to others.

One day a pastor whose church had just begun recovery group meetings cornered me to express his objections. "The big problem with some of these support group people," he blurted out, "is that they become so self-centered that they don't look beyond themselves." We were standing in the hallway of his church's office building and, sure that everyone in the area was hearing him, I was embarrassed.

"All they care about," he went on, "is their own lives and circumstances. They couldn't care less about what other people are going through." I kept shuffling closer to his office door, hoping he would invite me in so we could close it.

While his accusations have some validity, his statements were too intense. He was the same pastor who had said that his congregation didn't need any of this "support group stuff." The members in his congregation had their lives "together" and would get along fine without groups for "people in crisis."

I knew I had to acknowledge his concern, but I also had to encourage him to give the new support group in his church an opportunity to continue for several more months.

"You're right about the ways in which some folks get so focused on themselves, their issues, and their spirituality, that they have nothing to give to others," I said. "But there are some very healthy people who have gone beyond themselves. The ones I know are the most reliable and faithful people anyone could have in a church or community."

"How do these people get to be that way?" the pastor asked, as he finally relaxed a bit.

I reminded him of Step Twelve. I told him I realized this was an ideal and that not all group participants could meet this ideal right away. The ones who do Step Twelve do it because:

1. They receive Jesus Christ day by day and moment by moment. They take in all that He has to give to them. They gratefully accept His grace and initiative in their lives.
2. They make up their minds that they are needed and that they must serve others. They become convinced that they can do this service. Jesus said that they will do **"greater works"** (John 14:12). Paul says, **"I can do all things through Christ who strengthens me"** (Phil 4:13). They believe these passages and put them into action.
3. They know their gifts and talents, and they are open to where God wants them to use these. They go out and find their spot (which most likely is where they are already), beginning in their own homes, and then serving other family, fellow employees, neighbors, and acquaintances.
4. These people serve. They do little things. There is a time in this Twelve-Step process when they need to focus on themselves for a while. And then they need to move away from themselves and in a healthy way reach out to others.

Jesus Himself did this. The first thirty years of His life were spent in preparation for ministry. And then He moved out into the world.

Paul spent fourteen years in preparation and then moved out into a phenomenal ministry.

To get healthy, we all need a time of ''recovery'' every once in a while. And then we need to move out into the front lines sharing who we are and what we have been given.

Jesus Serves the Disciples

They were at their last supper together. His betrayer was at the table with Him, along with the other eleven disciples.

Jesus got up from the table, removed His outer garment, and took a towel and wrapped it around His waist. He then poured water into a basin and began to wash the disciples' feet and to wipe them with the towel He was wearing.

Peter said to Him, ''Lord, are you going to wash my feet?''

Jesus answered, ''At the moment you do not know what I am doing, but later you will understand.''

''Never,'' said Peter. ''You will never wash my feet.''

Jesus replied, ''If I do not wash you, you can have nothing in common with Me.''

When He had washed their feet and put on His clothes again, He went back to the table. ''Do you understand,'' He said, ''what I have done to you? You call me Master and Lord and rightly so—I am. If I, then, the Lord and Master have washed your feet, you should wash each other's feet. I have given you an example so that you may copy what I have done to you.

''I tell you the truth, no servant is greater than his master, and no messenger is greater than the man who sent him. Now that you know this, happiness will be yours if you do this'' (based on John 13:3–17).

1. The message for me from this reading is about
____ having faith (''You do not understand now, but you will understand.'').
____ servanthood.
____ being a model teacher.
____ learning how to wash the feet of others.

____ _____

2. The main reason I don't serve others more is
____ I don't know where the need is.

____ I don't know how to serve others.
____ I don't know how to begin. I want to serve, but I need help in getting started.
____ I don't have time for serving others. My hands are full already.
____ Serving others is not my gift.
____ Serving others is not a priority for me.

____ _____

3. If I had been Peter and Jesus had come to wash my feet, I
____ would have reacted just as Peter did—originally refused to let Jesus wash my feet.
____ would have died.
____ would have been very threatened by this act of servanthood. If Jesus did that for me, it would mean I would have to do the same for others.
____ would not have thought much about it. I would have simply let Jesus do as He had planned.
____ would have been very humbled by this experience.

4. To the best of my knowledge, here is my own assessment of where I am with the Twelve Steps:
____ They have helped me a great deal, especially with _____

_____

_____

____ I am now ready to serve others by reaching out to share the love of Christ with them.
____ I need another go-around with the steps. Right now I feel inadequate to reach out. I need more time. (Some people need years).
____ I am working at putting these principles to work on a daily basis. They are working for me.
____ I am eager to share what I have learned with others. I am looking for a place to do that.

Just as Jesus served others, He also asked his disciples to serve those who needed help.

The Young Man Who Was Called to Serve

A man came running up to Jesus, knelt before Him, and asked Him this question: ''Good Master, what must I do to inherit eternal life?''
Jesus said to him, ''You know the commandments; You must not kill; you

must not commit adultery; you must not steal; you must not cheat; you must not bear false witness; honor your father and mother.''

And the young man said to Him, ''Master, I have carefully kept these commandments from my earliest days. What is still missing in my life?''

Jesus looked steadily at him and loved him, and He said, ''There is one thing you lack. Go and sell everything you own and give the money to the poor, and you will have treasures in heaven. Then come follow Me.'' But the young man's face fell at these words and he went away sad, for he was a man of great wealth (based on Mark 10:17–22).

1. Why do you think the rich young man come to Jesus?
____ He was looking for another way to make money.
____ He was empty. He knew something was missing in his life.
____ He wanted to find a sure way to heaven.

____ _____

2. Which of Jesus' responses to the rich young man impressed you the most?
____ That Jesus looked steadily at him.
____ That Jesus loved him.
____ That Jesus told him how to solve his problem: go sell what he had and give the money to the poor.
____ That Jesus called him to come and follow Him.

3. Even though the rich young man had carefully kept the commandments from early in his life, one thing was still missing for him. What do you think it was?
____ His heart was not surrendered to God.
____ He was good and he was religious, but he had not ''sold out'' to God.
____ His wealth was an obstacle.
____ He did not have a relationship with Jesus Christ.

4. At this point in the Twelve Steps, what is the one thing that is still missing in your life?
____ My wealth is an obstacle for me.
____ I am not willing to sell everything I have and give the money to the poor.
____ Eternal life is not that big of a deal to me.
____ I don't have a good relationship with Jesus Christ.
____ I don't care much about poor people.
____ I am afraid to be ''sold out'' to God.

Jesus set these two examples for His disciples, and He also told His disciples to serve other people.

What the Bible Says about Step Twelve

Choose one passage from the selections given and read it each day during the next week. Think about how the passage might apply to you as you reflect on the choices given. As a final comment, write your own personal application of the passage to your life.

1. John 21:15–17—After His resurrection, Jesus showed up on the shoreline of Tiberias. He provided some bread and a fish dinner for the disciples after they had caught nothing on a fishing trip.

> **When they had finished eating, Jesus said to Simon Peter, "Simon, son of John, do you truly love Me more than these?"**
> **"Yes, Lord," he said, "you know that I love You."**
> **Jesus said, "Feed My lambs."**
> **Again Jesus said, "Simon, son of John, do you truly love Me?"**
> **He answered, "Yes, Lord, you know that I love You."**
> **Jesus said, "Take care of My sheep."**
> **The third time He said to him, "Simon son of John, do you love Me?"**
> **Peter was hurt because Jesus asked him the third time, "Do you love Me?" He said, "Lord, You know all things; You know that I love You."**
> **Jesus said, "Feed My sheep"** (based on vv. 15–17).

____ I am overwhelmed with this assignment of feeding sheep but know that Jesus will give me the strength I need.
____ I believe that Jesus knows all things
____ I love Jesus Christ.
____ I want to feed the sheep that He has called me to serve in my home, work, and church.

____ _____
____ _____
____ _____

2. Matthew 25:31–46—This is part of Jesus' teaching about the Last Judgment. It's direct and scary, but a healthy reminder of our responsibility to serve others.

When the Son of Man comes in His glory, and all the angels with Him, He will sit on His throne in heavenly glory. All the nations will be gathered before Him, and He will separate the people one from another as a shepherd separates the sheep from the goats. He will put the sheep on His right and the goats on His left. Then the King will say to those on His right, "Come, you who are blessed by My Father; take your inheritance, the kingdom prepared for you since the creation of the world. For I was hungry and you gave Me something to eat, I was thirsty and you gave Me something to drink, I was a stranger and you invited Me in, I needed clothes and you clothed Me; I was sick and you looked after Me: I was in prison and you came to visit Me."

Then the righteous will answer Him, "Lord, when did we see You hungry and feed You, or thirsty and give You something to drink? When did we see You a stranger and invite You in, or needing clothes and clothe You? When did we see You sick or in prison and go to visit You?"

The King will reply, "I tell you the truth, whatever you did for one of the least of these brothers of Mine, you did for Me." Then He will say to those on His left, "Depart from Me, you who are cursed, into the eternal fire prepared for the devil and his angels. For I was hungry and you gave Me nothing to eat, I was thirsty and you gave Me nothing to drink, I was a stranger and you did not invite Me in; I needed clothes and you did not clothe Me; I was sick and in prison and you did not look after Me.

They also will answer, "Lord, when did we see You hungry or thirsty or a stranger or needing clothes or sick or in prison, and did not help You?"

He will reply, "I tell you the truth, whatever you did not do for one of the least of these, you did not do for Me."

Then they will go away to eternal punishment, but the righteous to eternal life" (based on vv. 31-46).

What do you most need from the Lord after reading this passage?
_____ Lord, I need help in loving and serving these people.
_____ Lord Jesus, please lead me to those who are hungry, thirsty, naked, and imprisoned. I am willing to go to be with them.
_____ Lord Jesus, I need guidance in serving others. Please help me.
_____ Lord Jesus, there are so many needs, I don't know where to begin. So I have done so little. Show me the way to serve, Lord.

_____ _____

_____ _____

_____ _____

3. James 2:14–26—This passage from the book of James was a direct challenge to those who thought that they could coast into heaven. In James's day, apparently there were some lazy folk who didn't feel a need to give to or serve others. James lays it on the line with them.

> **What good is it, my brothers, if a man claims to have faith but has no deeds? Can such faith save him? Suppose a brother or sister is without clothes and daily food. If one of you says to him, "Go, I wish you well; keep warm and well fed," but does nothing about his physical needs, what good is it? In the same way, faith by itself, if it is not accompanied by action, is dead.**
>
>   **But someone will say, "You have faith; I have deeds." Show me your faith without deeds, and I will show you my faith by what I do. You believe that there is one God. Good! Even the demons believe that—and shudder. You foolish man, do you want evidence that faith without deeds is useless? Was not our ancestor Abraham considered righteous for what he did when he offered his son Isaac on the altar? You see that his faith and his actions were working together, and his faith was made complete by what he did. And the Scripture was fulfilled that says, "Abraham believed God, and it was credited to him as righteousness," and he was called God's friend. You see that a person is justified by what he does and not by faith alone. In the same way, was not even Rahab the prostitute considered righteous for what she did when she gave lodging to the spies and sent them off in a different direction? As the body without the spirit is dead, so faith without deeds is dead** (based on vv. 14-26).

_____ Lord, with Your help, I pray that my words and actions will be the same.

_____ _____

_____ _____

_____ _____

In all these passages Jesus is calling us to move beyond ourselves and reach out to others.

Beyond Self

I was fifteen years old when I first *heard* of the Twelve Steps. At that age, hearing about "steps" to anything, meant nothing. I was a typical teenager: I knew everything. I had an independent spirit. I was trying out my wings. I was tired of being told how to live life.

Through Al-Ateen and Al-Anon, I *saw* the Twelfth Step in motion. I saw people who lived out the Twelve-Step lifestyle. They talked about it and they lived it. When someone in their group had a need, they helped each other. They were there to support each other emotionally. They helped meet each other's physical needs. They stood by each other prayerfully.

I was involved with some Al-Anon people who invested much of their time, energy, and money in developing a great treatment center for chemically dependent people and their families. They served unselfishly. They were always available to share parts of their stories that might be helpful to individuals or families.

I saw people in pain reaching out to each other. Suffering families found hope in being with others who had similar problems. Individuals were sharing themselves and their stories with each other. Recovering alcoholics were going out to meet with active alcoholics to tell them their stories and to share the good news: that recovery is possible and there is another way of life.

"It's too bad there aren't more alcoholics" was the familiar comment from a close friend of mine. "Alcoholic families have two major advantages: (1) they have an identifiable problem; and (2) they have an excuse to get help with their problem. I wish all families could have the privilege of getting the kind of help alcoholics families can get," he said.

Seeing these folks' support for each other gave me a vision and model that have been deeply integrated into who I am. I have a clear idea of what the Christian community could look like.

My spiritual formation began in parochial schools. After opening my life to Jesus Christ, receiving Him, and developing a relationship with Him, I continued to grow in healthy, prayerful Catholic spirituality alongside solid, evangelical, scriptural growth. Subtly and gently, the Twelve-Step process has been there as a part of this growth. The Twelve-Step process is a natural part of Christian formation.

In my experience, all the previous eleven steps build toward this twelfth step. I am most alive and excited about life when I am sharing with others. When I am giving of myself to others, I feel best about myself. When I am exercising my gifts for the benefit of others, I am energized.

The twelfth step is an action step. It challenges me to give as others have given to me. All of us have made it this far because others have given to us. Now it is our turn to give in response.

This giving is not only material things; it is simple and small things. It involves holding a door, saying an encouraging word, complimenting someone, writing a note, phoning a friend, shoveling a neighbor's walk, or volunteering to chaperon for a school activity.

Step Twelve challenges us to leave the comfortable. It nudges us to move out into the hurting world to bring healing, light and Jesus Christ. He is the bread of life that all the world seeks. We are His hands and feet.

We must go beyond ourselves and our group. We must go—to love, to give, and to serve. Our problems were given to us as opportunities to grow and experience God's love and compassion more deeply—so that we can go out and share that love and compassion with others, just as we have experienced it.

Groups have a wide variety of outreach ideas. One Twelve-Step group decided to pool their resources, to go a neighborhood widow's home and paint her house. Other groups have taken up collections and contributed to others' needs. Individuals whose lives were transformed in Twelve-Step groups give to others in many ways.

Step Twelve is an action step. It's about doing, moving out, and going. We are to reach out and share with others that which has been give to us in love.

In some ways the first eleven steps are essentially preparation for Step Twelve—the first eleven free us up so that we can serve Christ and others.

To be a follower of Christ means we have chosen to deny ourselves, to take up our cross, to follow Him. Being a follower of Christ means more than being ''spiritual.'' Being a follower of His means we are ''into'' Christ, the Person, and He is ''in'' us, and we follow where He leads—into the world that needs us to share Him.

We have chosen a path of surrender and service. It is our way of life. We seek to love as we have been loved. We seek to serve as Jesus served us. We seek to put our faith into action.

Doing Step Twelve

I am grateful that God is changing me through these Twelve Steps. In response, I will reach out to share Christ's love by practicing these principles in all that I do.

Check below those areas that you personally will do something about:

____ Write a note to my parents.
____ Write a note to my spouse.
____ Offer to share my resources.
____ Volunteer my time to help where I am needed.
____ Write letters to lonely relatives.
____ Tell my friends about Jesus Christ.
____ Buy and take a Bible to them.

____ Write notes to my children.
____ Call someone to let them know I am thinking of them.
____ Start a group (or another group) like this.
____ Invite a friend to this group.
____ Write a note to a coworker.
____ Help a friend with a project.
____ Write a letter to a missionary.
____ Give someone some of my clothes.
____ Give something valuable away.
____ Give more money to my church.
____ Today, pray for everyone in this group.
____ Pray for one country in the world every day.
____ Make arrangements to visit someone in prison.
____ Give my friend a Bible for his/her birthday.

____ _____

____ _____

____ _____

____ _____

____ _____

____ _____

Check below those you think your group should do:

____ Invite others to come to the group.
____ Begin a second group (split this group).
____ A weekly collection. Give the money to_____.
____ Get each person in the group a Bible.
____ Support a mission(s).

    ____ local _____.

    ____ national _____.

    ____ international _____.

____ Go on a short trip together.

    ____ city (urban) _____.

    ____ mission _____.

____ Work on a project to help others.

___ Go visit shut-ins.
___ Adopt a grandparent.
___ Befriend a lonely or rejected child or teenager.
___ Visit a hospital.
___ Pray for my ministers and staff. Offer to serve them.

___ _____

___ _____

___ _____

___ _____

___ _____

___ _____

And there are greater ways in which we can give to fulfill the challenge of the twelfth step:

—Fulfilling our life mission
—Doing our best in our profession
—Serving others the best we can
—Taking risks in exploring ways to make better use of our lives, gifts, and talents.

These we work at one day at a time, one moment at a time.

As Christians, we have a clear call: to bring the message of Jesus Christ to others, all around the world. Missionaries have a call to serve others in a foreign land. We each have our own mission work. It may be someone in our church, our next door neighbor, or a distant relative. We have the wonderful privilege of handing on the good news to others: Christ is here. Christ is alive. Jesus loves us and accepts us just as we are. What more could anyone want?

My participation in small group meetings has given me more than I can comprehend. It has given me unconditional acceptance, affirmation, support, encouragement, new vision, and renewed hope. As I meet with a group that uses this framework, I am given the nourishment I need to go back out to my family, profession, and friendships. I am renewed and strengthened to love those I am with—even those who may sometimes be unlovable.

The Final Benefit of the Twelve-Step Process

As I approach my fifth decade of life, I am more aware than ever of the need for healthy, clear voices to speak in the darkness of our times.

Our culture needs women and men whose lives are well integrated, balanced, healthy, and congruent. These times demand more integrity from men and women than ever before in the history of America.

The world needs true disciples of Jesus Christ as it never has before.

True disciples don't become "true" by simply going to church, affirming a specific doctrine, or going to Bible studies. True disciples need more than that. They need a way to become whole, healthy, and integrated. They need a lifestyle based on and patterned after Jesus Christ.

We must all learn again what it means to be a whole person. We must all return again to those years when our grandparents held us in their arms, sat in rocking chairs, and told us simple stories. We need again that kind of parenting, encouragement, direction, and guidance. We need once again to discover sincere compassion—basic concern and caring for our families, neighbors, and others.

This book will draw us back into the basics. It will point us in the direction of the simple life. It will get us into a process that will make us more aware of our vulnerabilities and our need to express them to others. It will help us discern what life is really like for us.

We all need something like the Twelve-Step process. Without such a framework we will too easily become our own "gods," designing our lives and our own agendas as we think they should be. These other "gods" will eventually bring us down. We have no business trying to run our own or anyone else's life.

As we cited earlier in this book, the well-known poster cites two fundamental realities in life:

1. There is a God;
2. You are not Him.

This book and this process have hopefully been a simple reminder of those fundamental realities.

Jesus said that we should enter by the narrow gate, since the road that leads to hell is wide and spacious and many take it; but it is a narrow gate and a hard road that leads to life and only a few find it (see Matt. 7:13–14).

This Twelve Step process helps readers find the narrow gate. It encourages participants to stay on the "hard road." We are fellow travelers on this journey into life. We need each other and this process. It will hold us accountable for our past, present, and future life.

As you go forward into this process and become even more molded and shaped by the love and grace of Jesus Christ, it is my prayer that you will experience great relief, joy, and freedom as thousands of others and I have done.

Making Step Twelve My Own

This section provides you with a format for integrating your feelings, responses to questions, and what you learned from this step, the Scriptures, and your group meetings.

Date, day, and time of your writings:

_____

1. At this point in my life, the major area that I am working on (finding a specific person I can reach out to day by day):

_____

_____

2. Major insights I was given into my life through this step (I need to serve more.):

_____

_____

_____

_____

3. The scriptural passage that spoke to me most clearly in this step (Faith without works is dead.):

_____

    The one word that has been most important to me in this chapter (Serve—I need to serve others.):

_____

_____

4. The major discovery about Jesus Christ that I was given in this step (He has called me to go. After I've been with Him, He wants me to get out and serve others.):

_____

_____

5. My strongest feeling as I work this step (an urgency to get out and serve):

_____

6. The action I feel called to take as a result of working this step (Specifically, make a call today to an elderly distant relative. I will offer to help her with the maintenance in her home.):

_____

7. The good news for me in this step and these passages (I am privileged to be called and to serve God.):

_____

The Twelfth Step—Standing by the Door

Sam Shoemaker passed on the principles of the Twelve Steps to Bill Wilson. And Bill Wilson passed them on through Alcoholics Anonymous to millions of other people whose lives have been changed forever.

Shoemaker wrote a poem, ''I Stand By the Door'' which explained the meaning of his life. Please read this poem as you move forward with the Twelve-Step process.

I Stand by the Door

I stand by the door.
I neither go too far in, nor stay too far out,
The door is the most important door in the world—
It is the door through which people walk when they find God.
There's no use my going way inside, and staying there,
When so many are still outside and they, as much as I,
Crave to know where the door is.
And all that so many ever find
Is only the wall where a door ought to be.
They creep along the wall like blind men,
With outstretched, groping hands.
Feeling for a door, knowing there must be a door,
Yet they never find it . . .
So I stand by the door.

The most tremendous thing in the world
Is for people to find that door—the door to God.
The most important thing anyone can do
Is to take hold of one of those blind, groping hands,
And put it on the latch—the latch that only clicks
And opens to the person's own touch.
People die outside that door, as starving beggars die
On cold nights in cruel cities in the dead of winter—
Die for want of what is within their grasp.
They live, on the other side of it—live because they
have not found it.
Nothing else matters compared to helping them find it,
And open it
and walk in
and find Him . . .
So I stand by the door.[1]

---

[1]Helen Smith Shoemaker, *I Stand by the Door: The Life of Sam Shoemaker* (New York: Harper & Row, 1967), ix.

TWELVE-STEP PROCESS
GROUP LEADERS
RESOURCE MANUAL

There will probably always be a continued need for A.A., Al-Anon, Narc-Anon, and other groups directed toward a specific addiction or compulsion. At the same time there is a great need for Christ-centered support groups that deal with all kinds of issues and help people address compulsions, addictions, and phobias—not only those related to chemical addictions. The church is the ideal place to develop these groups.

How to Begin This Process

1. Read through the following pages for an overview of how to begin groups in your church, neighborhood, or community.
2. Continue to pray about this idea.
3. Ask your pastor for his/her approval and involvement.
4. Begin sharing this idea with others.
5. Follow the process suggested in this manual.

This manual was originally prepared as an outline for those participating in a group leaders training workshop. Training sessions are available. You can write for more information at the address at the end of the book. Although developed for use with Twelve Steps to a New Day, the information in this manual is valuable and transferable to any small-group process.

The Twelve-Step small group process responds to the real needs and pain of kids and adults.The Twelve Steps for Life in Christ break the cycle; change the pattern; and confront dysfunctional lifestyles

• through a gentle framework that models and invites sharing of real feelings.

191

- by inviting and encouraging talking.
- by fostering trust.
- by helping participants understand what is normal and abnormal behavior.
- by providing a safe, confidential environment.
- by giving participants true community (a much needed extended family).
- by providing a clear focus on the person of Jesus Christ.
- by letting participants feel that their worth comes from who they are, not what they accomplish.

How to Use This Process

When you begin a group, think in terms of an ongoing group for at least one year. Take one step each week. After you have gone through the Twelve Steps and when you get to the thirteenth week, begin again with Step One.

As you work your way through the steps, simply select one or two interactive exercises from the chapter/step you are on, and use that as a way to help participants share.

Always break into small groups of four for part of the meeting.

Consider having several groups each week (morning, afternoon, and evening options).

Introduce church members to the groups through a presentation given by a group member (see sample talk in this manual) and/or through a twelve-week series at adult forums or adult education or at twelve-week series of introductory comments at board meetings, council meetings, or other established gatherings.

Introduce this process through one or two annual retreats: Focus on one or two steps at each retreat.

Inform people in the community of ongoing groups available at your church or neighborhood gathering place.

Everyone Benefits from Participation in the Twelve Steps for Life in Christ

Leaders discover

> encouragement, a more centered life, a way to express their gifts, a group to belong to, support, spiritual growth, fun, revitalization, leadership and skills development, and more.

Group participants discover

> a safe environment to share within, nonjudgmental friends, support, encouragement, a lifestyle for growth, renewed spirituality, perspective, a way to look

at themselves freely and honestly, lifestyle models, a gentle ''system'' that brings wholeness and health, a solid biblical perspective, and more.

The sponsoring group or congregation realizes

renewed members, a place to refer people, growth, the development of skilled leaders, a core support group that affects the entire congregation with its caring perspective, hurting people cared for, revitalized spirituality, renewed focus on the basics and more.

A Way to Begin Groups

After you have shared all this with your pastor/leaders and have approval,

1. Gather names

   1. Names of those I think might be interested in co-leading this group with me:

      _____   _____

      _____   _____

      _____   _____

   2. Names of those I might ask to join me as part of a core group:

      _____   _____

      _____   _____

      _____   _____

      _____   _____

      _____   _____

   3. Names of those who might be participants in the group:

      _____   _____

      _____   _____

      _____   _____

      _____   _____

      _____   _____

_____   _____
_____   _____
_____   _____

2. Set the date, day and time for the meeting:

_____

3. Determine the place of meeting:

_____

4. Arrange for the room:

   • A smaller room is best.
   • Sit around a table if at all possible for the large group.
   • Use movable chairs for the small groups.

5. Your preference is to have a(n)   ____ open group.   ____ closed group.
   A closed group has a defined membership. The same people come most weeks. This type of group fosters intimacy more quickly but risks becoming cliquish. After becoming quite comfortable with each other, the group may be less likely to admit newcomers.
   An open group has changing membership. The number of people and the people in attendance can change from week to week. An open group is less intimate, but is more capable of welcoming and making newcomers a part of what the group is doing. Open groups are more likely to stay focused on the "task" —the steps—and could be healthier in the long run.
   My experience with groups is that the open groups ultimately are more effective. My bias is in favor of open groups.

6. Set a date for your first core meeting. Call to get books. (Every group participant needs a book to write in daily and weekly. It is usually best to order a supply of these to have on hand, distributing one to each person who comes to the meeting. We suggest that the book be a gift from the church or group, but if members would like to buy a copy, announce that they can do so).

7. Begin publicity (see section in this manual). Consider the possibility of having a "sign up" Sunday. Have a sign-up table at the back of church after each Sunday morning service for several weeks. Have a layperson give the sample talk, and

encourage people from the congregation to sign up. Or pass out forms during the church service and have people indicate whether they would like to participate or not and drop the forms in the collection plate.

Walking through a Meeting

Every group meeting is different. Each group approaches the meeting in its own unique way. Some of the consistent elements in a group meeting are listed below. Since these are suggestions only, please adapt them for use in your groups.

A Suggested Agenda and Time Analysis

- Welcome through Scripture reading, ten minutes
- Small group sharing, thirty to forty minutes
- Presentation/sharing, ten to fifteen minutes
- Closing and prayer, ten to fifteen minutes
- Suggested total meeting time: one and a half hours

Before the Group Meeting

What kind of group is it? Open or closed?

- Greeters at the door
- Table for literature
- Coffee and tea available
- Tables set up for groups to gather around

Opening the Meeting with the Welcome

Welcome to this Twelve Steps for Life in Christ group. We are here to support each other. Every one of us has certain areas of our lives that cause pain and questions. We have found hope in each other and in God. Through the Twelve Steps for Life in Christ, we are learning how to live life in a better way. For this we are thankful.

Through Jesus Christ we receive the courage we need to make needed changes in our lives. The group helps us to be honest with ourselves. We are here to help each other. We are doing this by sharing ourselves, gradually, as we become more comfortable with each other.

Please join us for several weeks before you make any final decisions about whether this group can help you. Rest assured that what you share here stays here in this room. All of us pledge to keep all of these conversations confidential.

Introductions (First Name) and Warm Up

Brief warm up/introductory exercise—Choose one of these: Rate Your Day; What Is Fun for You?; Your Favorite Room; Your Favorite Time of Day; One Satisfying Thing in Your Life Right Now; Your Best Relationship Right Now.

- Collection (optional) proceeds to go to _____ (order books; missions; send leaders to training; a contribution to the church)
- Read the Twelve Steps on p. viii-ix
- Read Serenity prayer on p. 56
- Read the designated Scripture passage for this step (choose any passage from the chapter).

Small Groups

- Choose one or several interactive exercises that will get the group started in sharing their feelings and experiences. (This is not a discussion group—it is a sharing group.)
- Assign four persons to a group (same group for six weeks).
- Designate which person begins and leads in answering questions in the interactive exercises
- Give a specific ''task''—identify the specific page number and the numbers of the exercises you want them to share about.
- Give a specific time for this sharing (thirty to forty minutes).
- Suggest prayer for one another now and throughout the week.
- Suggest contact with each other outside the group meeting.

Back to Large Group Gathering

Step Presentation is given by one of the leaders or a group participant. This sharing is based on the step, the scriptural passages for the step, and the person's own experience. These presentations are best when they focus on what the person is presently experiencing, relating the step and the presentation to his or her circumstances.

Wrap Up

- Announcements
- Suggested light assignment: specific page; specific questions to prepare for next week's meeting
- Updating participant calling list—pass the sheet around

• Prayer requests/sharing of answered prayer
• Very brief closing comment from the leader
• Closing prayer

Group Covenant

Group leaders may want to develop a group covenant with some or all of the following components. This is best done after the group has met for three weeks or more. Many small group trainers consider the covenant crucial to small group outreach.

Please adapt these components as you see fit.

The name of our group is _____.
We will meet at (beginning time_____) until (_____ closing time) each (day_____). The exceptions will be on _____.
We will meet for at least twelve weeks. After the twelve weeks we promise to be honest in evaluating this group. We may very well keep this group going for as long as it is needed.
We promise to be honest to the best of our ability.
We will pray for each other.
We will do our best to come prepared.
We promise to help each other.
We will listen to each other without interrupting.
For this twelve-week period we choose to be (check one)
_____ an open group (anyone can come from week to week).
_____ a closed group (we will have a select group that will come from week to week).

Date _____Signature_____

Please list and distribute first names and phone numbers of group participants.

The Leader's Role

Almost anyone can serve as leader of a Twelve Steps for Life in Christ group. Most leaders have learned a great deal through life experiences. Although they have much to offer, many leaders feel they have little . . . or that their lives must be perfect before they can lead a group.

"We minister best out of our weakness," is the familiar line. All the struggles of daily life are what make us, shape us, and mold us into mature human beings. The process and the impact of all those issues and struggles on our lives give us leadership abilities.

The essential resources for an effective Twelve Steps for Life in Christ group are

- A facilitative leader
- The Scriptures
- A clear focus on Jesus Christ
- The Twelve-Step framework
- The group and their willingness to share themselves

Ultimately you, as the Lord is in you and works through you, are the group's greatest resource.

Leaders, while in process themselves, are also

- Emotionally and spiritually mature
- Examples but not perfect
- Alive with the love and divinity of Christ, yet very human
- Encouragers, and sometimes needing encouragement
- In a trusting relationship with the Lord, even in severe difficulties (see 2 Cor. 4:7–18)
- Willing to pray for and with the group and individuals
- Committed to the Scriptures—not necessarily scholars, but recognize, in faith, that the Scriptures are inspired by God, the ''Bread of life,'' ''a lamp unto our feet.''

Good leaders let the Scriptures speak to them in their personal lives and in the group process. The Scriptures are our primary resource (2 Tim. 3:16–17).

This small group process is a way for all participants to get into the Scriptures and integrate them more thoroughly into their own lives.

The leader is a *servant*. Leaders lead by being honest, open, and appropriately vulnerable. Leaders adapt the material in this book to apply it in the most meaningful ways to the people who attend their group. Leaders *encourage* and nourish others. They work on finding the best in others, drawing them and their gifts out. Leaders also *set the tone* of the meeting by being themselves and encouraging others to do the same through modeling. Leaders *share themselves and Jesus Christ* with others in the group. This is done naturally, emerging from their life struggles and relationships and flowing out of the step for the week and the related readings.

On the practical side, leaders *facilitate* the meeting keeping it focused on one step, the designated readings, questions, and appropriate sharing. Leaders *keep the meeting on track*. Responding to the variety of personalities in each group meeting, leaders know how and when to ''intervene'' to call the meeting back to sharing.

- They begin and end the meeting promptly as scheduled.
- They are attentive to the group process (respect silence).
- They share feelings and experiences.
- They share how the step and readings apply to their own lives.
- They ask for logistical help (coffee, sitters, collections, bookkeeping, book orders).

Leaders also work with other leaders. Ideally, each group has two leaders, a male and female. Leaders have an ongoing relationship with the pastor(s) or person designated to coordinate this ministry with them.

Finally, leaders have fun, enjoy the process, and relax. The formation and development of a Twelve-Steps-and-Beyond group ultimately depend upon God. Relax and trust. Enjoy the process. Let it flow.

> **Unless the LORD builds the house,**
> **They labor in vain who build it.** (Ps. 127:1)

Write out your greatest concerns or fears about beginning or developing a nourishing small group.

I am most afraid of

_____

_____

_____

My greatest concerns are

_____

_____

_____

Prayerfully turn these over to God, let them go and trust that these fears and concerns will be addressed by Him.

Good News for Group Leaders!

This is God's work and ministry. You are His vessel. The success or failure of the group does not depend upon you, your skills, or your experiences. Our strength, courage, and nourishment to convene and lead groups comes from the Lord and our relationship with Him.

Please review these passages often. They will help you keep your leadership and ministry in perspective.

1. **"If anyone is in Christ, he is a new creation; old things have passed away; behold, all things have become new. Now all things are of God"** (2 Cor. 5:17–18a,). This is God's ministry. It began with Him. It belongs to Him, and He sustains it. As a leader, be faithful to your call. Let go of the results, and leave evaluation to God.
2. **"I have been crucified with Christ; it is no longer I who live, but Christ lives in me; and the life which I now live in the flesh I live by faith in the Son of God, who loved me and gave Himself for me"** (Gal. 2:20). This is the greatest of all miracles: Christ lives inside you. Your presence, as Christ is in you, is your greatest gift to others. Your "best ability is availability."

   Let go. Trust in the Son of God. He loved you and gave Himself for you.
3. **"To them God willed to make known what are the riches of the glory of this mystery among the Gentiles: which is Christ in you, the hope of glory"** (Col 1:27). As a leader, you know the secret things of God. Mostly you know that Christ is at work in and through you. Praise Him.
4. **"In Him dwells all the fullness of the Godhead bodily; and you are complete in Him, who is the head of all principality and power"** (Col. 2:9–10). You and all others seek fulfillment. What we seek we discover in Jesus Christ. He is our fulfillment. He is what we seek. As we discover this for ourselves, others in our groups will make the same discovery.
5. **"I can do all things through Christ who strengthens me"** (Phil. 4:13). This is our promise and hope. We need not do this or any ministry in our own strength. We can do this through Christ who strengthens us.

Twelve Steps for Life in Christ Small Group Leader Job Description

As a Twelve Steps for Life in Christ small group leader, I _____ (name), commit myself to the following minimums:

1. I promise to pray for each participant in my group on a consistent basis.
2. I will prepare for the meetings.
3. I will attend and participate in all the meetings (one and a half hours per week) except when I cannot, I will alert my co-leader so that he/she can prepare and lead the meeting in my absence.
4. I will attend meetings with other group leaders (one to two hours).
5. I will contact each person in the group outside of the group meeting at least once every twelve weeks.

Characteristics of Twelve Steps for Life in Christ Group Leaders

1. They are compassionate.
2. They are contemplative/prayerful.
   - Devote time to prayer each day.
   - Pray for the group.
   - Pray for the individuals in it.
   - Pray with others about the group.
   - Solicit the prayers of others.
   - Seek to learn and be at home with solitude.
   - Are at peace with themselves and the quiet places in their lives.
   - This is the growing and primary work of a group leader: To pray and solicit the prayers of others.
3. They are "articulators of inner events" (Henri Nouwen, *Wounded Healer*).
4. They are risk takers.
5. They are enablers/facilitators of others and their ministries.
6. They are persistent.
7. They are visionary.
8. They are biblically based (see Ps. 1).

Informing Others about Your Meetings

Personal invitation is the best way to get people to participate in meetings. Word of mouth always works best. Most people need several invitations, but persistence pays off.

Don't be discouraged by low attendance. Sometimes a meeting for two is very fulfilling. Sometimes it takes a year before the word gets out about your group and its importance.

To begin with, your personal calls to people are the key. Consider your contact and invitation an important end in themselves. Most people are flattered to be invited to participate in a group like this. In their loneliness and isolation, your call means a great deal to them. It can be an excuse to be with them in some of their struggles.

Consider the following outreach possibilities as supplements to personal invitations:

- A sample talk (below)
- Neighborhood newspaper article
- TV interview with group leaders
- Radio interviews
- Listing the groups in the church bulletin
- Contacting local counselors and clergy associations and letting them know that you have these groups
- Mailing/delivering a flyer to local churches
- Speaking at service clubs
- Speaking at PTA and other parent organizations
- Highlighting the step for the week in church bulletin
- Distributing ''business cards'' with dates and times of meetings

Here is a sample promotional talk that you or another lay leader of a group can adapt to your setting and needs.

I'm excited about something we are developing in our parish (congregation)/community—something that I have thought about for years. It is a process called the Twelve Steps for Life in Christ.

These groups are for men and women of all ages—married, single, or divorced. They meet on (dates) at (times) in (rooms). You are welcome. Everyone is welcome.

This group is for anyone who wants to grow and get healthier. It is not just for those with major problems. Many group participants deal with simple, everyday temptations and anxieties. In the group they find the help they need.

You may have heard of some of the good that has come from A.A. or other anonymous groups. The Twelve Steps for Life in Christ group follows a Twelve-Step format but is distinctive because Jesus Christ is identified as the ''higher power.'' We all need reminders about the presence, love, acceptance, and forgiveness of Jesus Christ. We all have one or several unmanageable areas in our lives. We all need more harmony in our lives—with ourselves, with other people, and with God.

This group is not a Bible study group or a counseling group. This is a sharing and support group based on biblical principles and the Twelve Steps. It is a group that provides a safe place for anyone to come to share about life's issues.

I have a need to be known for who I am. I want to know other people as they really are. More than that, I have a need to share with others my struggle to understand how God works in my life and the lives of others around me. I know that there are men and women in this community today who also have needs in their lives. Won't you please come to join us in this important, confidential gathering?

There are no dues, fees, or memberships. Simply come as you are.

Please call me or talk to me today. Brochures are on the tables in the back, and there is more information in the bulletin today.

A Scriptural Model for Community, Small Groups, and Outreach Ministry

They devoted themselves to the apostles' teaching and to the fellowship, to the breaking of bread, and to prayer. Everyone was filled with awe, and many wonders and miraculous signs were done by the apostles. All the believers were together and had everything in common. Selling their possessions and goods, they gave to anyone who had need. Every day they continued to meet together in the temple courts. They broke bread in their homes and ate together with glad and sincere hearts, praising God and enjoying the favor of all the people. And the Lord added to their number daily those who were being saved (based on Acts 2:42–47).

The Early Church as a Model for Community, Small Groups, and Outreach Ministry

1. It was a learning church:
   About Jesus Christ
   Their experiences about Him
   What He taught them
2. It was a praying church:
   Praise
   Seeking direction (dependence upon Him)
   Intercession for brothers/sisters
3. It was an alive church/things were happening:
   Results of the above—prayer, teaching
   Signs and wonders

4. It was a united church, "together"
   One purpose
   One mind
   One in spirit (personal agendas set aside)
5. It was a sharing church; they gave to anyone in need.
6. It was a worshiping church.
7. It was a growing church.

Growth was a by-product. Outsiders were attracted.

This is a model for our time. This is what our people are crying out for. This is the work of the church:

"That you believe in Him whom He sent [Jesus Christ]" (John 6:29) and **"To love one another so that the world will know we are His disciples"** (based on John 13:34–35). These are the objectives of small groups and the Twelve Steps for Life in Christ.

A Vision for an Integrated Ministry

The principles below can be applied to youth groups, Twelve-Step groups, small groups, and outreach groups:

1. This is a ministry of the heart (see Eph. 4:18), primarily
   Compassion
   Sharing
   Appropriate intimacy
   Meeting real needs
2. This is a ministry of prayer.
   Alone, together
   Contemplative
   Helplessness
   Healthy dependence
3. This is a ministry led by lay adults.
   They are available.
   They seek their ministry.
   They can make long-term commitments.
   They can start up easily.
   They are "wounded healers."
   Their needs:
       —training
       —ongoing nourishment

  —monthly support meeting

  —prayer

 The administration is simple.

4. A ministry of small groups within a large group context.

 The large group—the congregation as a whole

 The small group—this Twelve-Step group

 Small groups within the Twelve-Step group (a suggested ratio of one to four)

 Interaction throughout the week and between meetings

5. Thoroughly scriptural

6. Focused on Jesus Christ—He is worshiped, loved, and served

7. Congregational prayer

8. Continuous progression through the Twelve Steps for Life in Christ

Characteristics of the Twelve Steps for Life in Christ

1. Personal vs. programmatic

 Addresses personal needs

 Personal contact

 Program is the framework/adapted

2. Experiential vs. didactic/cerebral/theoretical

 Immediate application and integration

 Not just theory, but practical assessment of how factors fit or work

3. Formation vs. information

 Character development; molding, not just teaching "data"

 Process

4. Scripturally based and centered/primarily

 Permeates the day; sets the tone

 Asks different questions

 Brings clarity

5. Process vs. curriculum completion

6. Integration vs. compartmentalization

7. Means to an end (an excuse), not an end in itself

8. Jesus-focused vs. self- or issue-focused

9. Faith life (adventure) vs. "sight" life

10. Balance vs. intensity

11. Therapeutic (not therapy) and preventative

12. Sharing vs. discussion

A Suggested Training Process for Group Leaders

Check with your pastor for small group leader certification requirements. There are two major dimensions to leadership training:

A. The initial orientation/training—This workshop for group leaders is an important orientation to group process and the unique integration of the steps with the Scriptures.

B. Ongoing training—

1. All leaders need continuous nourishment and input. They need feedback, evaluation, affirmation, and direction. Meetings for leaders need to be held on a consistent (monthly?) basis.
2. Ideally, leaders are themselves in a Twelve-Step process where they are not required to lead. This is a support group for a leader.
3. Ideally all leaders have a "sponsor." Sponsors have also been described as mentors, soul-friends, guarantors, disciplers, encouragers, spiritual directors. The relationship is bound together in mutual love, care, and concern. This is important to avoid burnout and keep on the positive edge. It is also good for modeling to group members the concept of "sponsorship."
4. Have a training workshop for new and potential leaders twice each year. (Many potential leaders are group participants.)
5. Provide workshops/seminars focusing on specific steps or themes, using our associates for an evening, morning, half-day, one-day, or two-day event.

Some Suggestions—Do's and Don't's

1. Be sure to focus on one step at each meeting.
   Read the step.
   Read and integrate the scripture references.
   Have a step/Scripture presentation to share how that person applies the step and passages in life and how he/she feels about him/herself in this context. (Pass the presentations around—the sooner a participant shares part of his/ her story in small groups and with the whole group, the more committed the person becomes.)
2. Focus on Jesus Christ. Jesus is the center, not ourselves, our group, or our issues. Be sure the group integrates His person and relevant characteristics (love, forgiveness, acceptance, presence).

3. Know other referral resources (pastor, pastoral care people, counselors). It is best if you know who these people are and their counseling framework. It is crucial that these counselors be supportive of the Christ-centered perspective. Be confident that they will supplement the good work going on in the group. Ask for a pastor's help on this.

4. Relax.

5. Listen.

6. Don't push, teach (this is not a class, but a process), give advice, or "parent."

7. Don't "control" the meeting. Let it flow. You are in a facilitative role. Start and end the meeting. Let the Holy Spirit prompt participation and control the meeting. Step back and let the meeting happen.

8. Don't be the focal point of the meeting. (Group members should not look to you for approval or comment after sharing.)

9. If at all possible bring Bibles to the meetings. Get a supply of Bibles that are all the same translation. When making reference to scriptural passages, refer to page numbers. Do not assume that your participants know how to navigate in the Scriptures. (In fact, never assume anything about any group participant.) Help them to avoid embarrassment.

10. Do not put anyone on the spot to read. When reading, read as a group; if you prefer to have individuals read, please ask them if they would like to do so, fully acknowledging that some participants do not like to read aloud.

11. Do not put anyone on the spot to share. Always give the freedom to pass. (Some participants have come for months without saying anything.)

12. This is not a support group for the leader.

13. An ideal group size is about ten to twelve participants. An ideal small group size is four participants, with one person as facilitator. An occasional meeting of all groups and leaders from several congregations or the community will provide a format for celebration and encouragement.

14. Ask leaders to commit to leading a group for at least one year. That period of time is essential for the group to become established and known throughout the community.

15. Anticipate the main obstacle to involvement in this process: "Why do I need this kind of group if I am not in a crisis or chemically dependent?" Most people need this lifestyle (see Chapter 1).

16. Each participant needs to have a book. The book is a tool to help participants write their own life stories. Urge participants to write, draw, or doodle. At the beginning of the process do not be surprised by the

little preparation participants do. Give them time at each meeting to review or prepare responses to questions.

17. The first time that participants walk through these steps, anticipate an exploratory attitude and a more intellectual approach. It is only after going through the Steps for the first time that participants have an overview of the process and begin to grasp the depth and importance of actually ''working the steps.'' Don't expect too much. This lifestyle is subtly caught.

18. Anticipate fluctuating attendance. Do not assume this is a reflection on you or your leadership.

19. Think of this group process as an excuse to build long-term friendships. One of the main purposes of this process is to build real and lasting relationships.

20. Do not be anxious about finishing the book, lesson, questions, or section. The books have a great deal of material. This book is to be used many times. Pick, choose—tailor each meeting to the needs of participants. Let the book be your tool to begin the process. The objective is to help each other discover Jesus Christ and the depth in His word. Get into the Scriptures and concentrate on them as quickly as possible.

21. The Twelve-Step process is really a healthy platform for:

- Preventative sharing
- Contextual, wholesome evangelization (the simple basics of the faith in a way that meets real, identified needs)
- Concentrating on Jesus Christ the Person
- Seeing how the issues and circumstances in our lives can draw us into a closer relationship with God and others
- Bringing perspective to our lives (putting issues, worries, and concerns into their proper place)

What Makes the Twelve Steps for Life in Christ Distinctive?

For years, Christians have sought the renewal and depth that came from the A.A. communities. They wanted the benefits of A.A. along with clearly identifying Jesus Christ as the Higher Power. This identification does not negate the long-standing, life-changing work of A.A. or other groups that have broader appeal or concern with first-stage recovery. It is simply a matter of calling our Savior by His name, not to be divisive, but to be clear and specific for our own sake and for the sake of others who are sincerely seeking Christ.

We humbly use the name of Jesus Christ as He instructed us to do. Our group is founded upon Him. He is the foundation, the Way, the Light, the Bread of Life, the Truth. Life is rich and full because of Him and His presence in our lives. We celebrate His love and good works among us. We rejoice that we can say His name. He is our Savior—not our group, our "program," the Twelve Steps, each other, or ourselves. He is the power beyond and higher than ourselves.

To Him we admit our helplessness. We acknowledge Him as Lord.

Our motive for calling on Jesus is not to be controversial, but to provide others and ourselves the opportunity to share openly the "Name above Names."

For further study, consider the Book of Colossians, Philippians 2, and John 10—17.

The Group Process

Reflect on your own first group experience. Getting in touch with the feelings you had at your first group meeting will be helpful as you think of newcomers to your group.

The ideal group size is ten participants with two leaders. Break into three small groups of four for small group sharing. If the group gets consistently larger, begin meeting as a large group; split into smaller groups for small group sharing; close in the larger group. Eventually, consider splitting the group to begin a second one.

Groups sometimes have an enthusiastic beginning and some occurrence of slump after several weeks of meeting. It is best to meet continuously and consistently each week. This consistency is an important and clear message to the community that you will be there for them.

All meetings need a warm-up exercise.

Most groups get to or go through three phases:

1. History giving

    In this phase, each person shares some of who he/she is; some of what he/she's been through; what he/she is dealing with now; and what is drawing him/her to this group. This is generally the sorting-out phase: What is it that I really am going through or need to work on? Where am I now?

    This phase can take months, sometimes years. Many people have lived in denial or have been so numbed by their own pain that it takes a long time for them to unravel all of that and get back in touch with themselves. Before they can proceed to get healthier, they need to know where they are first.

2. Affirmation

In this phase group participants feel more acceptance and recognition for who they are—their feelings, their expressed values, their gifts. After going through the Twelve Steps one or two times, this becomes the settling-in phase for most participants. It is generally the phase of discovery and often "feels" positive and adventurous.

3. Goal setting

In this phase, group participants have identified their "core issues" more clearly; they feel encouraged to change; they feel support in wanting to make changes. In this phase participants begin to "contract" with self and others to work on areas of their lives that need resolution. This is one of the reasons why the steps are so helpful—they help participants move gently from one growth area to the next.

This goal-setting phase is the working, sometimes frustrating phase because changes don't seem to happen quickly enough. Ultimately new visions begin to get clearer in this phase.

There is no time line for any of these phases. Each individual moves at his/her own pace.

Occasionally, read the twelve assumptions below. They will serve as reminders about some of the basics of this group process.

Twelve Assumptions about Groups

1. Everyone, at all ages, can benefit from participation in a Twelve Steps for Life in Christ group. Most adults need a Twelve-Step group.
2. Every group participant is created in the image of God and has unused, unlimited potential.
3. As human beings, our potential finds its fulfillment in Jesus Christ and a supportive community.
4. Christian community is the result of commitment, common effort, time together, vulnerability, and sharing. The more risking and sharing, the more growth.
5. Personal growth begins internally. The freedom to risk comes through deeper intimacy with Jesus Christ and a supportive community.
6. The Holy Spirit has given every person gifts to share with others in the group.
7. The Scriptures are our guide for life.
8. Wellness and wholeness include every dimension of life—mind, body,

spirit, and relationships. The Twelve Steps touch upon and challenge us in all of these areas.

9. Celebration takes place when people are heard and feel understood, loved, and freed up through the love and power of Jesus Christ and the group.

10. We discover our true selves primarily by sharing with others.

11. We all seek to be known as we are, to know others as they are.

12. Jesus Christ has come to set us free and to bring us the abundant life. The Twelve-Step group process is a gentle system that gradually helps us to see Him and ourselves more clearly.

The Twelve Traditions for Life in Christ

These traditions should be read monthly at meetings.

1. Jesus Christ is our identified Higher Power. ''Jesus Christ is the visible expression of an invisible God'' (based on Col. 1:15).
   Our spiritual growth depends on faith in God and trust in Jesus Christ.

2. All men and women are in need of the presence, love, acceptance, and forgiveness of Jesus Christ. We are all human. We have all sinned.

3. In our group, there is only one ultimate authority, a loving God. God works through our group conscience and our group leaders. Our leaders are servants. They do not control or govern the meeting or group.

4. The Twelve Steps have universal application. Everyone's life has some unmanageable elements. The only requirement for participation in our group is a desire to grow.

5. Our group's purpose is to encourage each other as we struggle with life's issues and draw each other closer to Jesus Christ, the source of life.

6. Each group is self-supporting and does not accept contributions from any outside source.

7. Confidentiality is the foundation on which our group stands. What is shared in our meetings stays in our meetings.

8. Everyone attending a group meeting has the option to speak or be silent.

9. Prayer is an important part of our meetings, but everyone attending has the option not to pray, to pray silently, or to pray aloud.

10. There are no right or wrong answers in the group. Our group will not give advice or judge one another. We are committed to supporting one another. (There may be a need and time for confrontation but only as Jesus prescribed it be done in Matthew 18:15–18.)

11. Our common purpose is to grow in the likeness of Jesus Christ. Our bond and our unity will come from our focus on Christ and our love for one another.

12. The Twelve Steps are positive and hopeful. They acknowledge that we are in the process of becoming, moving toward the fulfillment that we seek.

Your Call to Leadership

Group leaders are needed to convene and facilitate meetings.

You can do this. You are needed to lead a group.

Our world is filled with people who suffer great pain. You can be the one who helps them begin a process of renewal, revitalization, and healing. Thousands, perhaps millions, have given praise for what Jesus Christ has done for them through small groups, the community, and the Twelve-Step process.

You are on the verge of a great adventure.

You already have most of the skills you need.

You already know most of what you need to know—your life experience has taught you that.

You are the greatest resource your group will ever have.

You have the ability to adapt resources to the specific needs of the people you will have in your groups.

This is your call to leadership. You can do this. You must do this. Others are dependent upon you to begin and continue this process.

*For more information on
training workshops,
retreats,
or a brochure on our
services,
please write*

Ron Keller and Associates

6104 Russell Avenue South
Minneapolis, Minnesota 55410
or call
612-920-8428